# Duck & Goose Cookery

To my husband, John,
The best friend any waterfowler could have

# Duck & Goose Cookery
## by Eileen Clarke

**Ducks Unlimted, Inc.**
Memphis, Tennessee

&

**Willow Creek Press**
Minocqua, Wisconsin

Book Design: Cecile Birchler
Cover Desgin: Monte Clair Finch

Published by Ducks Unlimited, Inc.
L. J. Mayeux, President
Julius Wall, Chairman of the Board
D. A. (Don) Young, Executive Vice President

ISBN: 1-57223-409-1
Published May 2001

DUCKS UNLIMITED, INC.
*The mission of Ducks Unlimited is to fulfill the annual life cycle needs of North American waterfowl by protecting, enhancing, restoring, and managing important wetlands and associated uplands. Since its founding in 1937, DU has raised more than $1.3 billion, which has contributed to the conservation of over 9.4 million acres of prime wildlife habitat in all fifty states, each of the Canadian provinces, and in key areas of Mexico. In the U.S. alone, DU has helped to conserve over 2 million acres of waterfowl habitat. Some 900 species of wildlife live and flourish on DU projects, including many threatened and endangered species.*

Library of Congress Cataloging-in-Publication Data

Clarke, Eileen.
    Duck & goose cookery / by Eileen Clarke.
        p. cm.
    ISBN 1-57223-409-1
        1. Cookery (Duck) 2. Cookery (Game) I. Title: Duck and goose cookery. II. Title.

TX750.5.D82 C57 2001
641.6'6597—dc21

2001024669

## CALL TO ACTION

The success of Ducks Unlimited hinges upon each member's personal involvement in the conservation of North America's wetlands and waterfowl. You can help Ducks Unlimited meet its conservation goals by volunteering your time, energy, and resources; by participating in our conservation programs; and by encouraging others to do the same. To learn more about how you can make a difference for the ducks, call **1-800-45-DUCKS.**

# CONTENTS

# CONTENTS

# CONTENTS

# CONTENTS

# ACKNOWLEDGMENTS

Many people have shared their knowledge, expertise, and products to make my work easier. Among them, I'd like to thank Pentax cameras, Tilia (makers of the Food Saver vacuum sealer),Cabela's catalog, and Chef'sChoice.

I'd also like to thank the state of Mississippi for its wonderful duck hunting; Aberdeen, South Dakota, Convention and Visitor's Bureau for their kind hospitality in the face of millions of snow geese;  and Pat and Nick Frederick of Ameri-Cana Expeditions, Edmonton, Alberta, for the best Canada and specklebelly goose hunting I've ever had.

# INTRODUCTION

This cookbook has been a labor of love. I am grateful for the necessity of wasting an entire rifle season chasing waterfowl, grateful to every friend who shared their variations on field care and aging techniques. Grateful for all the delicious waterfowl recipes my hunting partners, business associates, and even some perfect—but very generous—strangers shared with me. And grateful, then, to go home and pluck, cook, photograph, and eat the birds—every delicious morsel.

And, finally, I'm grateful that Gideon, my bird-dog-in-training, got to burn off a little of the terrible twos in a duck blind. When research can be defined as spending most of your frosty mornings and moonlit evenings at that incredibly fertile zone where land meets water, then life is more than good: it is a huge bite out of heaven.

As a consequence, this book is full of well-tested and delicious wild duck and goose recipes. No domestically raised birds were used, no wild bird wasted for the sake of a more technically correct photo. (If you need proof, turn to "Judy's Method." You'll notice the bird used in the photographs is minus a head. That's the way it came into the kitchen; that's how we photographed it.)

And all birds photographed were still edible—and in fact delicious—after the photo was taken. Like all bird hunters, I had to abide by possession limits and wanton-waste laws, cookbook or no cookbook. So if one or two of the photos in these pages don't exactly remind you of those you see in commercial gourmet magazines, there is a good, and ethical, reason.

In the process I have found, once again, that there are a lot of great and generous cooks hiding out in camo clothing. More than once these friends and hunting partners gave me first pick of the birds, so that these photos would be as beautiful as possible. From the cornfields of South Dakota to the delta country of Mississippi and back in my own backyard in Montana, I am grateful to all of these generous and sharp-shooting friends.

This book is a collection of recipes that range from the sublime to the exquisitely simple. But a recipe is only part of the equation when it comes to putting wild game on the table. Every hunter knows the work starts when the bird falls out of the sky. Therefore, I've included instructions on field-dressing birds, the when and how of plucking, information on packaging for a longer freezer life, as well as an illustrated guide to cutting up birds more easily—and sometimes more elegantly—for the table. Finally, I've offered suggestions for which recipes work best to hide strong-tasting birds and which to use so as not to overwhelm mild-tasting birds. There are marinades galore, and recipes for legs, that most difficult of body parts to cook. In short, everything you need to know after the shot to make the eating as rewarding as the hunting.

There is a danger in this book, of course. The danger is that after trying a few recipes, those people who have been so generous with their bounty in the past may become quite possessive of their birds. So if you, like me, need a little help filling the freezer, go make a date with a wingshooting instructor. And then be careful whom you give this book to. In the meantime, let's break out the pots and pans and get cooking!

DUCK

&

GOOSE

# TESTING THE WATERS

COOKERY

F EW THINGS ARE AS INDIVIDUAL AS TASTE. I lean toward buttered noodles. My husband, John, puts jalapeño peppers on everything. And my brother-in-law likes steak-and-kidney pie. Fortunately, we are at the top of the food chain; what we eat doesn't affect how we taste, or at least it doesn't matter. Not true for waterfowl. What waterfowl eat, and how the elements and human population growth treat them, greatly affects their own natural tendency either toward or away from culinary delight. To put it bluntly, grain-fed mallards dry roasted with a bit of salt and pepper taste great; then again, diving ducks on a diet of crustaceans and clams are stronger than a garlic milk shake.

How does the cook decide which recipe will work best for each bird? You start with knowledge of the habits of individual species, then keep an eye to the calendar and the state of feed in your hunting spot. Later, when you pluck the bird, check it over for age and fat content. Smell it, look at it, handle it with care, and cook it within 4-6 months. We'll talk about the care later. First and foremost, it's the bird. Let's start with ducks.

## IF IT WALKS LIKE A DUCK...

For the cook, there are two kinds of ducks: surface feeders and diving ducks. Of the commonly hunted ducks, mallards, black ducks, pintail, gadwall, wigeon, shovelers, and blue-winged, green-winged, and cinnamon teal are surface feeders. Surface feeders are also known as dabblers, tippers, puddle ducks, and river and pond ducks. They prefer freshwater, though they may spend some time in salt or brackish water during migration. What the casual observer sees is the typical "duck butt" in the water: a duck tipped over in shallow water or along the edges of lakes, ponds, and rivers, feeding only as far as its neck and bill can reach, with the latter half of its body still visible above the surface of the water. What the hunter notices is that surface feeders generally have larger wings and can pop off the water into immediate flight, not needing the running start that most diving ducks require. What the cook will notice about surface feeders is that a large percentage (up to 98 percent) of their diet is vegetation, and the vegetation they choose to eat creates a milder-tasting flesh.

The most commonly hunted diving ducks include red-heads, canvasbacks, greater and lesser scaup, ring-necked ducks, goldeneyes, bufflehead, scoters, and ruddy ducks. Divers are also known as bay ducks; because of their physical makeup they feed and breed in big water. They dive below the surface for food, disappearing completely and eating both vegetation and a variety of animals from the lakebed or riverbed. And while divers don't exactly reverse the percentage of vegetable matter to animal food in their diets, they eat enough mollusks, insects and insect larvae, crustaceans (including crayfish), and small fish to make their flesh rate somewhere between less palatable and off-putting, depending on the species. Bufflehead, for instance, eat about 80 percent animal matter, greater scaup over 50 percent, and goldeneye (both Barrow's and common) 75 percent.

Redheads and canvasbacks, though divers, have long had a reputation for great flavor, but that was before their favorite food came under attack. And while Mississippi pecans, for instance, still make that region's canvasbacks quite delicious, wild celery grass and eelgrass are an entirely different story. These were the principle coastal foods of cans and redheads that made their flesh the most highly rated among both hunters and shoppers in the market age. I still know people who trust that any canvasback or redhead they shoot—anywhere they shoot them—will be as delicious as the birds of their youth, and sometimes they are.

**AND IF IT TALKS LIKE A GOOSE . . .**
Like ducks, geese vary in taste, despite the fact that their wings and feet are generally consistent from Canada to snow to brant to Ross' goose. In the goose family, brant have the same taste for wild celery grass and eelgrass as canvasback and redhead ducks, though with wild celery in short supply, brant have adapted and learned to feed in grain fields. The curious thing is that they still enter and leave grain fields based on the tides. And while a low tide once made it easier to reach those wild celery roots, it is hardly an advantage in a grain field.

Snow geese have a reputation for being less tasty than Canadas, though both are heavily vegetarian. The rap on snows may have something to do with their habit of eating and traveling in much larger flocks, with the result that some birds are in prime, heavy grain, while others—perhaps less dominant birds—may not be. Their taste lately may simply be a result of their increased numbers, though the birds I brought home this fall were delicious.

## HOW DO YOU TAKE CARE OF BIRDS?

Traditionally, plucking a bird has always preceeded drawing the bird. That's because it's easier to pluck a bird when it's still warm than once it has lost all body heat. (And all but impossible to pluck one that is in rigor mortis.) The problem, however, is that I like to age every bird that is not badly shot up, because aging birds, like aging beef, makes the meat more tender. And while most birds you bring home are going to be young of the year, by the end of the season even they're pretty old and pretty tough. And how do you tell old birds from young ones, absolutely, infallibly?

I like them aged. But I also like my birds to be mild-tasting. That means, by necessity, that at our house we compromise. We split the drawing into two steps. The intestinal tract is the chief source of sour flavors, so step one is to remove any and all internal organs involved in processing food—from the upper and lower intestinal tract to the liver, gizzard, and craw—as soon as possible, most often in the field, at the end of the morning's hunt. We complete the second half of the drawing, removing the lungs, heart, esophagus, and other miscellaneous organs after the bird has been aged and plucked, 4-7 days after the bird has been taken.

If you want to balance mild taste with tenderness as we do, follow the directions below in the order listed, starting with the initial drawing, and rinsing as soon as possible. Obviously, the sooner the milder. If you prefer a stronger wild flavor, age your birds without drawing them, but be sure to examine the chest and belly feathers of the carcass for blood and the sour smell of intestinal juices. If the lower tract has been perforated by shot pellets, you will get a lot more flavor than you bargained for. And if mild taste is the sole consideration, skip to Arnie's saltwater soak method, in the "Variations on a Theme" section that follows.

Choose the method of game care that reflects the way you want your birds to appear—and taste—at the table. First, here are the specifics of our own efforts to find that delicate balance between mild flavor and optimal tenderness.

## STEP I: PARTIALLY DRAWING THE BIRDS

In the field, as soon as possible, make a small cut, starting at the vent, cutting forward toward the sternum, but only long enough to fit your thumb and index finger. The gizzard will probably come first, followed by the lower intestines—which should appear right at the hole, no matter how small it is. Grasp what you can of the intestines and pull gently but firmly. If the tract has not been perforated by shot, it should come out in one piece. Once the gizzard and intestines are

out, gently reach with your index and middle finger for any other internal organs you can reach easily, including the liver and heart. Now turn your attention to the bird's neck. Feel for the crop. It lies where the neck and breast come together. If it is full, the crop will be quite obvious under your fingers. Make a small slit in the neck skin—not through the crop membrane—and check its contents. If the crop is full of dry grain (wheat, barley, etc.), empty the contents on the ground. If the craw is full of anything else, including crustaceans, frozen vegetation, or snails, carefully remove it whole from the bird and discard it. Rinse the body cavity from the vent opening with clean cold water until the water runs out fairly clear. (You will finish drawing the bird after it has been aged and plucked.)

## COOLING THE BIRDS IN THE FIELD

Unless you're hunting in very cold weather, you will need to ice the birds as soon as possible. Place the birds in a cooler with a block of ice, and place the cooler in the shade. Remember that with waterfowl you are not only dealing with radiation heating on a cool day, but with the birds' own very effective feather insulation. Cooling is a bit harder to accomplish with waterfowl—particularly late-season, heavily feathered waterfowl—than with upland game birds.

Once you are home, and ready to age them, rinse the birds again. Then arrange the feathers to cover the small slits you made to draw the birds, and place them in a plastic bag. Both measures will protect the birds from drying out.

DOUBLE-DUTY STUFFED MUSHROOM CAPS
*recipe page 15*

CHILI FRESCA
*recipe page 32*

**WATERFOWL CARNITA**
*|recipe page 78*

**DELICIOUSLY DIFFERENT
CROCK-O-LEGS**
*|recipe page 79*

**DEEP-FRIED
WHOLE CANADA GOOSE**
*|recipe page 47*

**MILLENNIUM STIR-FRY**
*|recipe page 76*

HOT PINEAPPLE KABOBS
*lrecipe page 73*

HARVEST DINNER
*lrecipe page 64*

**CHORIZO IN A BLANKET**
*lrecipe page 94*

**BOCKWURST & FRIED POTATOES**
*lrecipe page 102*

**CATCH-ALL CASSOULET**
*|recipe page 28*

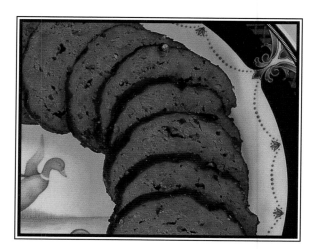

**OVEN SALAMI**
*|recipe page 103*

DUCKS-ELLES IN
PHYLLO BASKETS
*|recipe page 18*

SMOKY DUCK SOUP
*recipe page 35*

MAKING STUFFING:
TRADITIONAL STUFFED
DUCKS
*|recipe page 39*

TOSTADITAS
*|recipe page 20*

**OSAGE-SMOKED MALLARD
WITH RED CABBAGE**
*|recipe page 112*

**GRILLED JALAPEÑO BREAST**
*|recipe page 62*

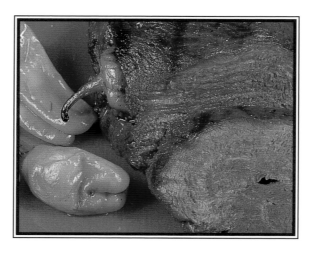

DEEP-FRIED WHOLE CANADA GOOSE
*recipe page 47*

DUCK RANGOON WON TONS
WITH SWEET-AND-SOUR SAUCE
*recipe page 19*

**SMOKED MEATLOAF**
|*recipe page 120*

**CURRIED DUCK**
|*recipe page 71*

**SWEET-AND-SOUR DUCK**
*|recipe page 74*

**DUCK ITALIANO**
*|recipe page 83*

## STEP II: THE SECOND HALF OF DRAWING

For best results, this step should be completed after the bird has been aged, plucked, and prepared for the freezer. (You can also complete the process just after the kill if you want really mild birds, but I don't recommend it, because that second opening at the neck allows a lot more air to circulate inside the bird, drying the meat out more.)

To finish drawing the organs: Rub your finger along the inside of the bird, between the rib cage and the spine, separating the lungs (they'll look pinker than the other organs, and more like bubbles than the solid maroon of livers and hearts) from the back of the skeleton. Then feel all around inside the body cavity. You should feel nothing but bone structure.

Now examine the neck opening. Remove the crop (if you haven't already) and esophagus, including the ballooned-out section where the quack and honk originates. They lie where the neck and breast come together. Once all the organs are removed, rinse well with cold water. You should be able to insert the tap into the neck opening and have the water flow freely and cleanly out the other end. If not, check for more internal organs. Then make one final check, rubbing a wadded-up paper towel inside the bird, especially along the inner rib cage and sternum. This will wipe away any residue of organs or blood.

My sister called me one Christmas morning when a great horned owl had beheaded one of her Guinea fowl. Her question was simple and panicked. She'd never cleaned a bird before, having used her little covey of Guinea hens to keep her alpacas bug-free, and she wanted to know, "How do I know when I'm done?" Guinea hen, pintail duck, or Canada goose, you're done when you feel only bony structures inside the carcass and the rinse water runs clean.

Note to those who had their birds "drawn" at a lodge: Before you put your birds in the freezer, or cook them, be sure to complete this last stage of drawing them. Lodges routinely leave heart, lungs, liver, and esophagus in the carcass when they prepare your birds for transport. So check both inside the body cavity, and then in the neck opening.

## AGING BIRDS IN THE REFRIGERATOR

Now that you've completed the drawing, it's time to add a little tenderness. And to keep peace in the family—and the refrigerator free of fuzz—it's best to wrap the birds first.

The bottom shelf of most refrigerators is a pretty cool 38 degrees Fahrenheit, which is a very safe temperature for aging. Allow the birds the maximum time: 5-7 days. But be sure to subtract the time it took you to get them home—on ice. If you don't have room enough in the fridge, find a place that is consistently cool: optimal aging temperature ranges from 33 F to about 45 F. Early in the season, the problem is keeping the birds cool enough; later, keeping them from freezing. (Aging stops cold when the birds freeze. No pun intended.)

If you have an old refrigerator—i.e., one that isn't frost-free—place the birds in a paper sack, fold the top over, and lay them on the bottom shelf of your fridge. For newer, frost-free refrigerators, use a plastic bag, and be sure to tie it or tape it shut. The difference is in the refrigerator. The newer frost-free models have very low humidity—it's one of the reasons they are frost-free—and for aging purposes tend to dry out birds. Thus a plastic sack, twisted closed, preserves moisture. If you have no room in the refrigerator, and don't have a spare, you'll need to find a safe alternative.

I live in a very old house that was moved in the late 1950s. The result is the character of an old house with a lot of "modern" conveniences. My favorite is the cement stairway that leads from ground level, outdoors, down into the basement. It features a pair of storm doors parallel to the ground, as in tornado country, which make the stairwell a perfect place to age birds—once I've run out of room in the refrigerator. It stays cool because it's outside of the house proper, but the semi-warmth of the basement prevents that vestibule from freezing easily. And I can control the temperature, if it

Clockwise, from bottom right: Duck breasts soaked in a dry white wine marinade, 1 percent milk marinade, red wine, and buttermilk (top right). As you can see, both wine marinades succeeded in tenderizing, and the 1 percent milk drew out some color (and wild flavors). It is the buttermilk that combines to provide both milder taste and tenderness.

gets too cold, by opening the basement door a crack. That's the kind of place you need. A garage with a wood or gas stove will also work. Just find a place that is cold without freezing.

## THE WONDERS OF BUTTERMILK

No matter what you do in the field, and no matter how well you take care of the bird getting it home, sometimes Mother Nature is not kind to the cook. Once in the kitchen, there are still a few things you can do to tame wild flavors and tenderize tough cuts.

One of the easier things to do is hide the wild taste in a heavily seasoned dish. The other thing is to do a pre-marinade, and what I've found works best is milk or buttermilk. Milk will leach out the off flavors in many wild meats, but the additional acids in buttermilk also provide a very effective tenderizing action. When using waterfowl for delicate-tasting dishes like the Pintail Piccata (page 67), let the meat sit in the buttermilk overnight—one cup buttermilk per pound of meat in a resealable plastic bag is about the right proportion. Then, rinse thoroughly before cooking.

Marinating those divers in buttermilk first can turn a salvage job into an Epicurean success, but if you are not fond of even the milder waterfowl flavors, a buttermilk marinade can also transform a good cut of meat into a great cut. It's like first aid for the kitchen. ■

If you can't get the temperature down to 33-45 degrees F, shorten the aging time accordingly. And if you simply can't get the birds hung at less than 55 degrees, it's best to just process them as soon as possible.

I think waterfowlers are some of the most inventive people. Take my friend Tim. Last year he had to replace the refrigerator in his reloading shed. From the outside the new fridge looks like any other kitchen appliance. But when you open the door, the first thing you notice is that the only shelf in there is at the top, just under the freezer compartment. Hanging from that shelf are about twenty metal S hooks where he can hang, and age, ducks. He keeps cans of pop and iced tea in the vegetable crispers for when friends drop by, but he converted the body of that appliance into the perfect meat cooler. I may have two more chest freezers than Tim, but I'm jealous beyond words of his second refrigerator. So are my birds, when they have to share space with the salad dressing.

# VARIATIONS ON A THEME: HIGH AND LOW FLAVOR

### THE SALTWATER SOAK

Here's a good way to remove blood from bloodshot meat, in birds not suitable for plucking whole.

Arnie Goldade, a taxidermist and sportsman in central South Dakota, has a lot of friends. One of the reasons he has a lot of friends, aside from his warm personality and straight shooting, is his shop. With its long, low work tables, deep sinks, and endless selection of boning and fillet knives, it's the perfect place to gather after a day of bird hunting to clean the birds. Did I mention that his method is totally different from mine?

He starts off by skinning out the birds and taking the breasts and legs off as soon as they get to his shop. Then he carefully trims and rinses the parts, and drops them into a five-gallon plastic bucket filled with an icy-cold light-brine solution. He takes the loaded bucket out to his unheated shed and places a gallon milk jug (filled with water and frozen solid for just this purpose) into the bucket. He lets this sit overnight, in the shed, at about 30 degrees. The next day, he removes the bird parts, rinses, dries, and then vacuum seals them. And into the freezer they go, less than 24 hours after the kill. And no handling the guts.

Aside from getting birds from field to freezer in less than 90 minutes, what did Arnie gain with this ice bath? Mildness of flavor.

Arnie started doing this ice bath to leach out the blood from bloodshot meat. I watched him prepare pheasants this way, and the change was dramatic. Legs and breasts that had had large discolored purple areas the night before were pale and delicate looking after 12 hours.

Arnie does this brine bath with all of his birds. And though the appearance in waterfowl—before and after—is nowhere near as dramatic looking as with the pale-meated pheasant, the taste difference is the same. If you've been cutting bloodshot meat away and discarding it, give Arnie's method a try. You won't get the tenderizing effect of aging, but bloodshot is bloodshot. At that point, repairing the flavor of the birds is more important than tenderness. You can always use these birds now for long, slow-cooked dishes and not dread the taste—or waste meat.

For small batches, add about 1 teaspoon of salt to a gallon of very cold water. Place in a deep bowl, or jar, and set in the refrigerator overnight. For larger batches: In a five-gallon bucket, add about 2-3 tablespoons of salt and breasts and legs of about 15 birds.

The temperature, though, is crucial. Keep it just about freezing, in the bottom of your refrigerator; or outdoors, in a safe place, when the nights are cold, and with a gallon carton of ice to keep the temperature stable. (And it's important to keep the ice contained in a sealed jug of some sort, so it doesn't dilute the brine solution if the ice melts a bit.

It's much more obvious on a pale-breasted pheasant. On the left, a pheasant breast clearly shows the leaching effect of Arnie's saltwater bath. The darker breast on the right was untreated. The effect on the flavor of geese and ducks is just as good, though not as clearly visible.

If Arnie's main goal is to tame wild flavors, the next variation works in the opposite culinary direction.

## AGING FOR "HIGH" FLAVOR

If you are one of those people who enjoy a richly flavored bird, aging is a good way to add to the flavor your waterfowl were born with. The traditional European way to age birds is to hang them by the neck, feet down, and leave them at 35-45 degrees F until the body separates from the head and falls to the ground below. How long it takes for this to happen depends on the age of the bird, the ambient air temperature, and other factors (including humidity). The advantage to this method is that there's no guesswork. You just keep an eye on the bird, and when he says he's done, he's done. (Rather like one of those pop-up buttons on a commercial turkey.) Then you proceed to pluck and draw the bird as above.

Before you try this method, think about one thing, though. When this method of hanging and aging birds was developed, there were no refrigerators, there were no antibiotics, and there were no health department inspectors removing tainted meat from the market. In those days, people had developed a certain amount of immunity to tainted meat—unless it killed them, of course, removing the weak from the gene pool. In short, we are, for the most part, not descended from those who were sensitive to it. Around the turn of the century, when Europeans were pouring into this country (including three of my own grand-parents) we still had that protection.

The problem is that for the last 60-70 years, and intensely for the last 50 years, U.S. government agencies and animal growers themselves have worked very hard to provide a clean and healthy food supply to American consumers. So, while this may have been an adequately safe way for our grandparents to age meat, we may not be as suited to eat it this way today.

If you have used this method all your life and never gotten ill—and I know people who have—then by all means age your birds this way. However, if you are just starting out as a hunter, and think you'd like to try it: Don't.

Anyone who wants to add flavor to their game meat should move it indoors—into the refrigerator—where the lower, consistent temperature makes aging wild birds safe.

## HOW SHOULD I COOK THIS BIRD?

Wild animals, be they encased in fur or feathers, have less fat than their domestically raised brothers and sisters. That is true whether the animal is a chicken or a domestically raised mallard. So when you go to cook wild meat, it's a good idea to ignore any directions written for the tame, hand-fed variety. Don't cook wild meat to the point that it is a medium-well or well-done gray color; don't cook wild birds to 185 F on your meat thermometer; and please don't parboil ducks before roasting. Conversely, don't be afraid to let a whole-roasted wild bird sit 10 minutes before carving it. Goose or duck fat will not magically transform itself into mutton tallow. (Unless it was mutton tallow in the first place.) On the other hand, follow the suggestions for freezer life, and don't keep your water-fowl over through the next season. In fact, if they're all gone by the second or third barbecue of summer, that's a good thing.

The two best ways to cook a prime, low-fat piece of wild meat is to quick cook it—either grilled or roasted—on a hot fire until the meat is rare, or at most just on the medium side of medium-rare; or long, slow, and wet. Why? Because wild animals, if they have any fat, store it where it will do it the most good: on the exterior of their bodies. Domestic animals are so fat they stuff the excess riches in and between the muscle tissue—marbling, in other words. Marbled meat, when cooked to well-done, is capa-ble of providing a constant stream of rendering fat to baste the muscle tissue so your beef steak, chicken, turkey, and pork loin doesn't completely dry out. Wild meat has no such marbling, but by cooking your duck slow and long or taking it off the grill before all the pink is gone you will keep the meat as moist and tender as nature meant it to be. ■

Leave the bird intact (i.e., do not draw it), follow the directions for aging in the refrigerator, and trim away any off-color meat before preparing the bird either for storage in the freezer or immediate cooking.

Either way you age your birds, you can tell when they've achieved the maximum benefit by pulling at the lower belly feathers. If they pull easily (rather like testing for ripe pineapples by pulling the leaf at the center top of the fruit), remove the birds from the fridge, let them come to room temperature, and pluck.

Note: For complete information on plucking, skinning, wrapping, and freezing, refer to the appropriate chapters at the end of the book.

DUCK

&

GOOSE

# APPETIZERS

COOKERY

# SNOW GOOSE TENDER CHUNKS

MAKES 24 BITES

### INGREDIENTS

$^1/_2$ cup flour

2 eggs, lightly beaten

1 cup crumbled Ritz crackers
   (about 24)

8 ounces breast meat,
   in $^3/_4$-inch cubes

Some of my favorite recipes have come from fellow waterfowl hunters. This one comes from a friend in South Dakota who gets lots of practice at both shooting and cooking all kinds of waterfowl. Use ducks or geese: mallards, snows, Canadas, or teal. They'll all cook up quickly, and stay moist and delicious with this 3-step coating.

### COOKING

1 Place the flour, eggs, and cracker crumbs in 3 separate bowls. Dry the cubed meat with paper towels.

2 Preheat a deep fryer, filled with canola or peanut oil, to 375 F. (A Fry Daddy will do the job.) While the fat heats up, dredge the cubes first in the flour, then in the eggs, and roll gently in the cracker crumbs.

3 Carefully drop the coated cubes into the hot oil, several at a time (leaving lots of elbow room between the pieces). Cook about 1-2 minutes, until golden to dark golden brown. ❖

# SKEWERED TEAL WITH ITALIAN SAUSAGE

**MAKES 4 8-INCH SKEWERS**

## INGREDIENTS

2 teaspoons dried rosemary

2 cloves minced garlic

1 teaspoon dried leaf oregano

$\frac{1}{2}$ teaspoon salt

$\frac{1}{2}$ teaspoon pepper

Boned breasts of 2 teal

$\frac{3}{4}$ cup red wine

$\frac{1}{4}$ cup oil

1 yellow onion, cubed

1 green pepper, cubed

4 ounces cased Italian sausage

French bread, in 2-inch cubes

Delicious dinner on a stick, with only one drawback. It's marinated. So get the marinade mixed up tonight, and tomorrow we dine. And if you're really thinking ahead, use your own waterfowl Italian sausage (page 90).

### PREPARATION

1 Mince the rosemary and garlic together, then mix with the oregano, salt, and pepper. Dry the teal breasts with paper towels. Roll the meat in the spice mixture, coating on all sides, and place in a resealable plastic bag.

2 Refrigerate for 1-2 hours. Then mix the wine and oil together and pour it into the bag. Rotate bag a few times, and place back in the refrigerator overnight.

### TO COOK

1 Drain the teal, reserving the marinade. Slice the breasts into 2 or 3 pieces, and thread them onto the skewers, alternating with chunks of onion, green pepper, Italian sausage, and French bread.

2 Preheat a propane grill, then turn down to medium. Or start 40 charcoal briquettes. Adjust the coals or propane accordingly.

3 Grill the skewers, turning and basting occasionally with the remaining marinade, 5-8 minutes, until the sausage is no longer pink.

4 To serve, remove the meat and vegetables from the skewers. ❖

# CHEESY WATERFOWL DIP

MAKES 2¹/₂ CUPS

## INGREDIENTS

2 tablespoons oil

1 pound ground duck/goose meat

8 ounces grated pepper Jack
   cheese

4 tablespoons whipping cream

2 teaspoons beef bouillon
   granules

¹/₂ teaspoon red pepper Tabasco
   sauce

Crackers

Here's an appetizer you can keep warm in the Crock-Pot until the duck hunters come home. And, no matter how cold the blind, I promise this medium-hot dip will warm them up in minutes. Add more Tabasco at your own discretion.

### COOKING

1 Heat the oil in a large skillet, over medium heat, and brown the ground duck/goose meat. Remove from heat.

2 Turn a Crock-Pot onto low heat, and transfer the browned meat to the Crock. Then add the grated cheese, cream, bouillon, and Tabasco sauce and stir all the ingredients until well blended. Cover the Crock-Pot and cook on low for about 20 minutes, or until the cheese is melted. Serve with crackers or toast squares. ❖

---

### GROUND MEATS

To me, legs and wings are the source of real variety in cooking waterfowl. You can use them whole in Crock-Pot recipes or parted out in slow-baked, juicy dishes. But the best choice (once you've breasted out the bird) is boning all the other meat for the grinder. Then you can make sausages, won tons, smoked meatloaf, cocktail meatballs, and a host of other dishes. For more ideas, check out the "Quick & Dirty" section beginning on page 140.

Once you get hooked on these dishes, you may end up wanting to grind the whole bird. Not that there's anything wrong with that. I've been known to grind up really strong-tasting ducks—whole—and then add an equal amount of ground chicken to it, to mellow out the flavor. ■

# DOUBLE-DUTY STUFFED MUSHROOM CAPS

MAKES 32 CAPS, PLUS 1 CUP CHIP DIP

## INGREDIENTS

1 packet ranch salad dressing
& recipe mix (1-ounce size)

16 ounces sour cream

Potato chips

8 ounces ground duck/goose
meat

32 small- to medium-sized
mushrooms

The great thing about a recipe like the Double Duty is that it's so versatile. You can follow these directions for 32 caps—plus dip—make 64 mushrooms for a big party, or just make a handful of caps. Each 1-ounce packet of ranch dressing mix holds 4 tablespoons of mix. So you can halve or even quarter the recipe, then adjust the rest of the ingredients and have exactly what you need—no more, no less. Helps that it tastes great, too.

COOKING

1 Preheat oven to 375 F. Combine the ranch powder with the sour cream per packet directions. For 32 mushroom caps, split the mix in half. Set one half aside in a dip bowl for the potato chips. In the other half, stir the ground duck/goose meat. Mix thoroughly, and set aside.

2 Remove the stems from the mushrooms. Gently wash and dry them. Set each mushroom cap down on a cookie sheet, and fill each with 2 teaspoons of the duck/goose mixture. Place in the center of the oven and cook 12 minutes, until filling is light brown.

3 Serve with other appetizers, or for fancy occasions add 1 table-spoon each of minced cucumber, minced green onion, and minced parsley. ❖

# SPICY PIN-BALLS

**MAKES 40 MEATBALLS**

### INGREDIENTS

**FOR THE SAUCE**

1 cup ketchup
1 tablespoon honey
1 tablespoon molasses
1 tablespoon soy sauce
2 cloves minced garlic

**FOR THE MEATBALLS**

$1/2$ cup bread crumbs
$1/4$ cup milk
8 ounces ground pintail leg
    meat
8 ounces ground skinless chicken
1 tablespoon dried onion flakes
1 teaspoon garlic salt
$1/2$ teaspoon ground cumin
$1/2$ teaspoon chili powder
$1/8$ teaspoon cayenne pepper

Make this appetizer as written, or make it up a day ahead of time and stick both the sauce and meatballs in a mini Crock-Pot in the fridge. Next morning you just need to plug it in (on low). No mess, no fuss on the big day.

### COOKING

*The sauce*

1 In a small saucepan, combine the ketchup, honey, molasses, soy sauce, and minced garlic. Bring to a bare boil, on medium heat, then cover and simmer 20 minutes over very low heat.

2 Remove from heat and set aside.

*The meatballs*

1 Meanwhile, preheat the oven to 450 F. In a small bowl, toss the bread crumbs into the milk, and set aside.

2 In a large bowl, combine the ground meat, onion flakes, garlic salt, cumin, chili powder, and cayenne pepper. Stir until well mixed. Then shape into meatballs about 1-inch in diameter (larger meatballs require more cooking time), and place on a lightly greased cookie sheet, in a single layer.

3 Bake until meatballs are golden brown, and no pink remains, about 8-10 minutes. (Cut one meatball in half to check.)

4 To serve, reheat the sauce, about 2-3 minutes, until it just starts to bubble, then gently roll the meatballs in the sauce and arrange in a serving bowl. ❖

# BOUDIN BLANC SAUSAGE WITH TARRAGON SMOKE

MAKES 2 POUNDS

## INGREDIENTS

1¼ pounds ground duck/
    goose meat
¾ pound pork butt, ground
2 slices white toast
½ cup cream
½ cup cooked white rice
1 cup diced white onion
2 teaspoons salt
1 teaspoon white pepper
2 eggs
½ teaspoon dried summer
    savory leaves
¼ teaspoon dried thyme leaves
¼ teaspoon dried basil leaves
¼ teaspoon dried tarragon
    leaves
1 bay leaf, crumbled
4-5 sprigs fresh tarragon
    (at least 5 inches long)

This is a great appetizer on a summer's evening when you've got lots of food being prepared and nothing on the table yet. In fact, I like it so well that I've started growing French tarragon (that's the edible kind) in my kitchen window. But whatever you can find at your local grocery will do: fresh basil, oregano, or marjoram are quite delicious.

### PREPARATION

1 Grind the meats together with the fine plate on your meat grinder. Cover and refrigerate.

2 In a blender, purée the dried toast into crumbs. Pour into a bowl with the cream and set aside to soak. In a large bowl, combine the rice, onion, salt, pepper, eggs, savory, thyme, basil, tarragon, and the crumbled bay leaf. Add the toast and cream mixture to the onion and seasonings, and stir well to combine.

3 Add the ground meat to the seasonings, mix thoroughly by hand, then stuff into hog-sized casings.

### COOKING

1 Start 4 dozen charcoal briquettes, or preheat a propane barbecue. When the briquettes are white-hot or the propane unit has been preheated and turned down to medium-high, wipe the sausages with a little oil.

2 Lay the tarragon sprigs on the coals just under the sausages, as you lay them on the rack. Cover the grill and open the bottom and top vents part way to keep the fire hot. Cook the sausages 15-20 minutes, turning occasionally to brown all sides.

3 To serve, remove to a platter, and slice into 1-inch slices. Use colored toothpicks to pick up and eat. ❖

# DUCKS-ELLES IN PHYLLO BASKETS

MAKES ABOUT 40

### INGREDIENTS

¹/₄ cup butter

2 tablespoons finely chopped
onion

1 clove minced garlic

4 ounces minced duck meats

2 ounces shitaki mushrooms,
chopped

2 tablespoons Madeira

1 tablespoon flour

¹/₄ cup heavy cream

¹/₄ teaspoon salt

Phyllo pastry (thawed 12 hours
ahead, in the refrigerator)

Make these tasty treats with commercially sold shitaki mushrooms, or with your own hand-picked morels. Those rich, nutty flavors will enhance just about any duck or goose flavors.

### COOKING

**1** In a large skillet, melt the butter over medium heat. Sauté the onion and garlic until softened, about 2 minutes, then add the duck meats, mushrooms, and Madeira, cooking until the pan is almost dry.

**2** Sprinkle the flour over the mushrooms, and toss until the flour disappears. Add the cream and salt, stirring constantly, and continue cooking until all the cream is absorbed. Remove from heat and let cool to room temperature. All this should take no more than 8-10 minutes.

**3** On a flat, cool counter, unfold 1 or 2 sheets of the pastry, and cut into 3-inch squares. Cover the rest with plastic wrap to keep it moist.

**4** Preheat oven to 350 F. Layer 4 of these squares, each layer brushed with butter (or lightly sprayed with oil) on top of each other. Then place 1 teaspoon of mushroom-duck mixture in the center of each layered square. Fold up corners, and twist. (No seal needed; it will stay in place.) Place on cookie sheet, and cover the oven-ready squares with saran wrap to keep moist.

**5** Bake until phyllo dough is just golden, 12-15 minutes. Slide off the cookie sheet (use a spatula if needed) and let cool 10 minutes on a wire cake cooling rack before serving. ❖

**TIP** If you, like me, live somewhere that causes phyllo dough to be transported long and far, you may find it harder to handle than the package directions describe. In that case, just make your layered 4-inch squares, roll them into mini-cigars, and bake as above. It won't be the classic basket, but the flavor will be just as rich and delicious.

# DUCK RANGOON WON TONS WITH SWEET-AND-SOUR SAUCE

MAKES ABOUT 60

### INGREDIENTS

**FOR THE SAUCE**

6 tablespoons pineapple juice

2 tablespoons brown sugar

2 tablespoons hoisin sauce

1 tablespoon rice wine vinegar

2 teaspoons cornstarch

**FOR THE WON TONS**

8 ounces diced or ground duck
meat

8 ounces cream cheese,
softened

1 teaspoon prepared creamy
horseradish

2 green onions, chopped

1 pound package won ton
wrappers

Peanut/canola oil for fryer

I love finger food, and this is one of my favorites for parties. You can either fill and fold the won tons and keep them refrigerated until you're ready to cook and eat them, or just go whole hog and hold the finished won tons in a 250 F oven for up to an hour.

PREPARATION

*The sauce*

**1** In a small bowl, combine the pineapple juice, brown sugar, hoisin sauce, vinegar, and cornstarch. Stir to dissolve the cornstarch.

**2** Microwave on high (700 watts) for about 1 minute, or until the sauce starts to boil and thicken a bit. Set aside. (Sauce is best at room temperature.)

COOKING

*The Won Tons*

**1** In a food processor, combine the duck meat, cream cheese, and horseradish. Process until the mixture is just chopped, pulsing off and on 1-2 seconds at a time, 4-5 times. When done, add the chopped green onion and stir in by hand.

**2** Place the won ton wrappers on a cutting board, 4-5 at a time. Place 1 teaspoon of filling in the center of each. Lightly moisten the edges of the wrappers. Then fold in half, corner to corner, so you have a triangle. Fold the long ends together, moisten the corners, and press to seal. Repeat until you're done.

**3** Preheat the oil in the fryer. (Temperature should be around 375 F for best results.) Cook the won tons in batches, without crowding, until crisp and golden brown, about 2 minutes, turning once to brown evenly. Drain on paper towels as you proceed with the next batch.

**4** To serve, dip in sweet-and-sour sauce. ❖

# TOSTADITAS

**MAKES ABOUT 40 BITE-SIZED SNACKS**

### INGREDIENTS

2 tablespoons oil

4 ounces ground duck/goose

¼ cup minced onion

1 tablespoons chopped green
   pepper

1 minced clove garlic

⅜ teaspoon chili powder

¼ teaspoon salt

¼ teaspoon ground black pepper

2 tablespoons sour cream

6 corn tortillas (5-6 inches
   diameter)

2 ounces grated Cheddar cheese

### THE SALSA

1 cup chopped ripe tomatoes

½ cup chopped yellow onion

½ teaspoon (canned) chopped
   jalapeño pepper

2 teaspoons chopped fresh
   cilantro

The best kind of finger food for the holidays, or for a quiet afternoon once the season is over. But make lots: These mini-tacos will disappear like Canada geese do when you finally get a day off.

### COOKING

**1** In a large skillet, heat the oil over medium heat and brown the ground meats. Add the onion, green pepper, and garlic and sauté until softened. Add the chili powder, salt, and pepper. Turn the heat off and add the sour cream. Cover and set this aside.

**2** Prepare the salsa: Chop the tomatoes coarsely, and add to the onion, jalapeño pepper, and cilantro. Mix well.

**3** Preheat the oil in a deep fryer. Cut the tortillas into 8 pie segments: in half, then in half twice again. When the oil is hot, dip each segment into the hot oil and fry until crisp, about 3-4 minutes each. Drain on paper towels.

**4** To assemble: Spread some of the meat mixture on the tortilla chips, then a bit of the shredded cheese, and top with the salsa. ❖

# GRILLED DUCKS WITH SPICY RASPBERRY SAUCE

SERVES 4

INGREDIENTS

1/2 cup raspberry preserves
1/2 cup diced green onion
4 teaspoons apple cider vinegar
4 teaspoons soy sauce
1 teaspoon garlic powder
1 teaspoon salt
Breasts of 4 mallards

I like my duck juicy and somewhat pink inside. If you like yours more on the well-done side, just cut your strips thinner. It will take the same time but will be a bit more cooked.

PREPARATION

At least 24 hours ahead, combine the preserves, onion, vinegar, soy sauce, garlic powder, and salt in a bowl. Mix well, cover, and refrigerate.

COOKING

1 If you are using wooden skewers, place them in water to soak for 30 minutes. Then start the fire. For propane, preheat the grill on high for 10 minutes, and turn down to medium-high heat. For charcoal briquettes, start 4 dozen briquettes and wait 25 minutes. Meanwhile, slice the duck breasts into 1x1 inch thick strips and thread onto the skewers.

2 Place the duck skewers on a lightly oiled cooking rack, and cook the birds until medium-rare, about 3-4 minutes a side, turning often. Serve hot, dipped in chilled raspberry sauce. ❖

# HIDE-AWAY PÂTÉ

MAKES 1 CUP PÂTÉ

## INGREDIENTS

4 ounces breast meat

1 tablespoon oil

4 ounces softened cream
   cheese

4 teaspoons onion powder

1 teaspoon garlic salt

1 teaspoon ground white pepper

Like a lot of great recipes, this one began as a mistake. My friend Rob sautéed up a couple of duck breasts, and the kids wouldn't eat them. Not wanting to waste hard-won game meat, he checked out the refrigerator, threw a few things together and—voila! Good food. The best part is that over the years Rob has used this same recipe for some of the scariest-tasting ducks he's shot, and served them to hunters and non-hunters alike. So, go ahead. Use the worst duck in your freezer. The cream cheese and spices will cure (almost) all ills, and provide a delicious party pâté or duck blind spread.

## COOKING

**1** In a heavy-bottomed skillet, sauté the duck breasts in the oil until well-done. Cool, then purée the meat in a food processor until finely shredded.

**2** Add the softened cream cheese, onion powder, garlic salt, and white pepper to the puréed duck and process until blended. Serve on pumpernickel cocktail bread, or toast cut into triangles. ❖

# DUCK LOVER'S PÂTÉ

MAKES 4 CUPS

---

INGREDIENTS

1 pound teal breast meat

2 tablespoons oil

1/4 cup puréed jicama

1/4 cup sour cream

2 teaspoons green jalapeño
    Tabasco sauce

1/2 teaspoon salt

1/2 teaspoon black pepper

Tortilla chips

---

I love the duck breast pâté on the previous page, but it is definitely a winter dish. Replacing the cream cheese with jicama (pronounced hick-ah-ma), a delicate, crisp vegetable used in Mexican cooking, lightens this appetizer up so it's perfect for summer patios and white corn tortilla chips. Choose a jicama a little larger than your fist, then cut the leftovers into strips—like carrot strips—and add to your salads or raw veggie trays.

COOKING

1 In a heavy-bottomed skillet, sauté the duck breasts in the oil until well-done. Cool, then purée the meat in a food processor until finely shredded. Transfer to a medium-sized bowl and set aside.

2 While the duck cools, purée the jicama: Peel and chop about 1/2 of the jicama into 1- to 2-inch chunks, then place in food processor. Measure the jicama and return just 1/4 cup of the puréed vegetable to the processor bowl. Then add the shredded duck, sour cream, green pepper sauce, salt, and black pepper and process until well blended. Serve with tortilla chips and cold Mexican beer—with lime wedges. ❖

DUCK

&

GOOSE

# SOUPS
# STEWS
# & CHILIES

COOKERY

# WILD RICE, MALLARD, AND MUSHROOM SOUP

SERVES 2-4

## INGREDIENTS

2 cups chicken bouillon

1/2 cup raw wild rice

1/2 ounce dried chanterelle
  mushrooms

3 cups warm water, in all

4 tablespoons butter, in all

1 1/2 tablespoons slivered
  almonds

1/2 cup minced onion

1 clove garlic, minced

1 teaspoon dried rosemary

1 teaspoon dried leaf thyme

5 tablespoons Madeira

2 teaspoons beef bouillon
  granules

4 ounces breast meat (1 side of
  1 mallard), in 1/2-inch cubes

I love intensely flavored one-dish meals. And I love the nutty, warm, stick-to-your-ribs quality Madeira gives this one. Serve it as a quiet anniversary meal for two, or as the first course of a holiday meal. It's special enough for either occasion. If you don't have mallards, use any dabbler. And if you can't find Madeira, as I often can't in my hometown, a medium-dry sherry will work almost as well.

## PREPARATION

1 Bring the chicken broth to a boil in a 2-quart saucepan. Add the rice, cover, and return to a boil. Immediately turn heat down to low and simmer, about 45 minutes, until the rice is tender and all liquid is gone.

2 In a small bowl, cover the mushrooms in 1 1/2 cups of the water, and let sit at room temperature until the mushrooms are soft, about 20 minutes. Drain the mushrooms and save the liquid. Dice the mushrooms.

## COOKING

1 Melt half the butter in a heavy-bottomed 3-quart pot over medium or high heat. Add the mushrooms and almond slivers and sauté until the mushrooms are golden, about 5 minutes. Transfer to a small bowl.

2 Melt the rest of the butter in the pan, and sauté the onion and garlic until soft, about 10 minutes. Crush the rosemary and thyme between your palms (or in a small food processor) and add to the mixture. Stir until you smell the herbs, then add the Madeira and let it simmer 2-3 minutes. Combine the last of the water with the beef bouillon granules. Add beef bouillon and the reserved mushroom

liquid to the pot. When it comes to a boil again, add the breast chunks, and stir to completely coat them with the stock. Bring the pot back to a simmer, turn down to low, cover, and simmer for 20 minutes or until the breast meat is tender.

**3** Stir in the cooked wild rice and the mushroom-almond mixture and let simmer, covered, for another 15 minutes to heat thoroughly. Serve with a hard-crusted Italian bread. ❖

---

### DEGLAZING THE PAN

While this wild rice soup doesn't use the technique of deglazing, it is a basic step in most soups, stews, and gravies, including Wine Glazed Tender Chunks (page 29), Dutch Oven Goose Stew (page 30), and many other recipes herein..

Deglazing the pan is a two-step process. Deglazing itself is simply adding liquid to the cooking juices left from roasting or browning meat. We all do it when we brown or roast meat, then add bouillon or cooking wine to start make a sauce (for stews, soups, or chili) or a gravy. And whether you add enough liquid to make a 5-quart soup, or just a splash, the purpose is to soften and incorporate the "tasty bits" into the sauce. Those tasty bits stuck to the bottom of the pan are caramelized bits of meat that add an incredible richness to our recipes. But there's the other step of this 2-step process.

That step is to dry the meat well before sautéing or browning it. If you don't dry the meat first (chunks, breasts, legs, whatever), the excess moisture will be released into the pot, creating a gray foamy liquid that cools the browning process, dilutes your sauce, and prevents the formation of those caramelized tasty bits in the first place. So, dry the meat. Then, when you're done browning, deglaze the pan, stirring up all those intensely flavorful and concentrated pan juices into your sauce. ■

# CATCH-ALL CASSOULET

SERVES 6-8

INGREDIENTS

3 pounds assorted bird legs

2 tablespoons oil

1 tablespoon butter

1 teaspoon sugar

$^1/_2$ cup Madeira

1 teaspoon chicken bouillon
   granules

$^1/_2$ cup water

2 tablespoons minced fresh
   parsley

1 teaspoon dried summer
   savory

2 cloves garlic, minced

$^1/_2$ teaspoon salt

$^1/_2$ teaspoon pepper

1 onion, sliced thin

2 15-ounce cans great northern
   beans

6 ounces kielbasa, $^1/_4$-inch slices

If you are a "generalist" like me and hunt a lot of different upland birds, too, eventually you end up with an assortment of legs that—individually—won't make anything large enough to feed a sparrow. Thus a catch-all recipe for assorted game bird legs. Why in a water-fowl cookbook? Because the waterfowl legs add a rich flavor to the pot that no other legs provide. PS: Feel free to throw in a cottontail as well.

COOKING

1 Rinse legs in cold water and pat dry. In a large skillet, sauté the legs in oil, butter, and sugar at medium heat until golden. Place in the bottom of the Crock.

2 Combine the Madeira, bouillon, water, parsley, savory, garlic, salt, and pepper. Pour over the legs. Layer the onions and beans, then top with sausage slices.

3 Cover the Crock-Pot and cook on low for 8 hours. Serve with a good hard-crusted bread. ❖

# WINE-GLAZED TENDER CHUNKS

**SERVES 2-4**

## INGREDIENTS

1 pound skinned breast meat,
   in 1-inch chunks

2 tablespoons butter

2 tablespoons olive oil

1 teaspoon salt

1/2 teaspoon pepper

1 cup finely chopped onion

1/2 cup red wine (Merlot or
   Cabernet)

1/4 cup sour cream

2 teaspoons cream-style
   horseradish

This recipe grew out of my addiction to horseradish. I put it in potato salads, coleslaw, hot soups, and have let it take over the herb section of my garden. (Right now, it's going head-to-head with an out-of-control pair of chive plants.) The thing with horseradish is that despite its bite, it's a very delicate flavor. Add it in the beginning of the cooking and the flavor goes up in smoke. Add it at the end with the sour cream and cook it just enough to get the whole dish hot again, and it lends an incredibly tangy edge to this dish. It will help to premeasure all your ingredients and start the water boiling for pasta when you start sautéing the meat: this dish cooks up very quickly.

### COOKING

1 Lightly brown the meat in the oil and butter mixture, over medium-high heat, for 3-4 minutes, turning once. Season with salt and pepper, add the onion, and continue to sauté until the onions are soft (another 3-5 minutes).

2 Deglaze (see sidebar on page 27) the pan with the red wine, and turn heat down to simmer. Continue cooking until the wine is reduced by half, about 7-8 minutes. Combine the sour cream and horseradish in a small bowl, and add to the pan. Stir to coat the meat with the pan juices, and cook until the mixture just comes to a simmer again. Serve immediately over fettuccine. ❖

# DUTCH-OVEN GOOSE STEW

**SERVES 6-8**

## INGREDIENTS

1/4 cup flour

1 teaspoon dried leaf oregano

1 teaspoon dried leaf thyme

2 tablespoons dried minced
   onions

1 teaspoon salt

1/2 teaspoon white pepper

2 pounds skinned goose breast,
cut into 1-2 inch chunks

4 tablespoons vegetable oil

1/2 cup red wine (Chianti or
   Paisan)

2 cups beef bouillon

1 teaspoon Worcestershire
   sauce

2 cups water

1/2 cup raw barley

1 pound carrots, quartered

I love thick sauces. My husband likes thin. So when he isn't watching, this is the way I cook. I dredge the meat in flour before cooking it, ensuring that I'll have a thick, smooth sauce to support all of these distinctive flavors. You can use this method anytime you're browning meat for a stew, and never again have lumpy or, worse, thin sauce.

## COOKING

1 In a large plate, combine the flour with the oregano, thyme, minced onion, salt, and pepper. Dredge the goose meat in the seasoned flour. In a 5-quart Dutch oven, brown the meat in the oil, in stages, over medium-high heat. Deglaze the pot with the red wine and start preheating the oven to 300 F.

2 Transfer the browned meat back to the Dutch oven, and add the bouillon, Worcestershire, and water. Stir to mix thoroughly, and add the barley. Now layer the carrots across the top of the pot. Cover and place in the oven. Cook 90 minutes to 2 hours, until the meat is tender. ❖

*bland — not good*

# HARD CIDER STEW

SERVES 2-4

## INGREDIENTS

4 cups hot water

½ teaspoon salt

½ teaspoon celery salt

½ teaspoon pepper

½ teaspoon paprika

½ teaspoon dried onion flakes

¼ teaspoon garlic powder

3 teaspoons beef bouillon
   granules

2 tablespoons oil

1 pound breast meat,
   patted dry

2 cups sliced zucchini

1 cup chopped celery

1 medium onion, quartered

2 bottles hard apple cider
   (9.3 ounces or 275 ml each,
   medium sweet)

6 medium red potatoes,
   quartered

This is one of those necessity recipes. I had a garden with potatoes, onions, and zucchini coming out my ears, and too many birds in the freezer to start a new hunting season. But the topper was when I bought a 4-pack of hard apple cider thinking it was regular—but high-quality—non-alcohol apple cider. The answer? Cook it. Cook it all and let the guests sort it out. What was once a problem became a favorite recipe.

### COOKING

1 In the hot water, dissolve the salt, celery salt, pepper, paprika, onion flakes, garlic powder, and beef granules and put aside. In a large Dutch oven, heat the oil over medium-high heat and brown the meat chunks well. When the meat is well browned, add the zucchini, celery, and onion and toss them in the pan juices. Allow them to soften slightly in the pan.

2 Add the cider and deglaze the pan. Add the bouillon and spice mixture and the potatoes and stir gently to mix. Cover and cook on the lowest heat possible for 60 minutes, minimum. Like all soups and stews this is better the second day. ❖

# CHILI FRESCA

SERVES 2-4

## INGREDIENTS

¼ cup oil

1 pound breast meat

2 cups diced onion

8 cloves garlic, minced

1 teaspoon salt

1½ teaspoons ground cumin

1 teaspoon dried leaf oregano

1 teaspoon dried leaf marjoram

½ teaspoon chili powder

½ teaspoon red pepper flakes

¼ teaspoon cayenne pepper

2 14.5-ounce cans whole
    peeled tomatoes

2 cups beef bouillon

2 15-ounce cans pinto beans

1 cup minced cucumber

2 tablespoons minced fresh
    cilantro

⅓ cup minced green onion
    (just the greens)

The cilantro thrown in at the end of this recipe is one of the things that makes this chili taste so fresh. But like everything fresh, cilantro is hard to keep. The best way I've found to prolong its life is to treat it like cut flowers. Soon as I get home, I take the cilantro out of the wrapper and rubber bands, cut off the bottom inch of damaged stems, and place the cilantro in cold, clean water. Change the water every couple of days, and if the cilantro was quite fresh to start with, you can keep it up to 3 weeks.

COOKING

1  In a deep saucepan, heat 3 tablespoons of the oil over medium-high heat. Brown the sliced meat in the oil, and remove from pan. Add the rest of the oil, then the onions, garlic, salt, cumin, oregano, marjoram, chili powder, red pepper flakes, and cayenne, and lower the heat to medium. Sauté, stirring frequently, until the onions are soft, about 3-4 minutes.

2 Return the meat to the onion mixture in the pot; add the tomatoes, bouillon, and beans. Lower the heat to simmer, stir the pot well. Then cover and let simmer 45 minutes, until the meat is quite tender.

3 In a small bowl, combine the minced cucumber, cilantro, and green onion. Set aside, at room temperature, until ready to serve the chili.

4 To serve, pour soup into individual bowls, top each serving with 2-3 tablespoons of the cucumber mixture, and eat immediately. ❖

# BLIND CHILI

SERVES 8

## INGREDIENTS

1½ pounds cut up duck or
   goose meat

3 tablespoons oil, divided

2 cups chopped onions

1 cup chopped celery

1½ cups beef bouillon

¼ cup red wine vinegar

1 can (14 ounces) red
   enchilada sauce

½ teaspoon ground cumin

½ teaspoon dried leaf oregano

½ teaspoon garlic salt

1 cup frozen corn (thawed)

1 15-ounce can kidney beans

Picture it: You're in a duck blind at 20 below, the wind is howling, and the snow is coming in so hard it's pitting your left cheek. And for lunch you have a cold sandwich, coffee, and a handful of Oreo cookies. Wouldn't you rather have a hot thermos full of stick-to-your-ribs chili made from the very birds you're hunting? Talk about following through. But beware: This chili is guaranteed to warm your belly.

COOKING

1 In a 5-quart Dutch oven, brown the meat cubes in 2 tablespoons of the oil over medium-high heat. Transfer to a platter and keep warm. Add the onions and celery to the pot with the last tablespoon of oil, and sauté until the vegetables are softened (about 4-5 minutes).

2 Return the browned meat to the pot, and add the bouillon, red wine vinegar, and enchilada sauce. Stir to coat everything, and add the cumin, oregano, garlic salt, corn, and beans, and stir one more time. Cover and bring to a low boil. Then lower the heat so the chili just barely simmers, and cook about 90 minutes. If you can't get your chili low enough to just simmer, place the Dutch oven in a 300 F oven and let it cook there. ❖

# MARSALA OVEN STEW

**SERVES 6**

### INGREDIENTS

1 pound duck or goose meat,
    cubed

¼ cup flour

2 tablespoons oil

1 yellow onion, sliced thin

5 cloves garlic, minced

1 teaspoon dried thyme leaf

1 teaspoon dried basil leaf

½ teaspoon dried rosemary,
    crushed

½ teaspoon white pepper

¾ cup Marsala

3 cups beef bouillon or broth

⅔ cup raw white rice

1 cup frozen mixed vegetables,
    thawed

The perfect answer for a busy day. This soup goes together in a matter of minutes, and slides into a moderate oven to cook while you go off and do something fun. Use a 5-quart cast-iron or enamel-lined cast-iron pot, so the cooking will be truly care free. And don't skimp on the Marsala. It adds a rich, luxurious flavor to all wild meats and is especially good with duck and goose.

### COOKING

1 Dredge the cubed meat in the flour. In a 5-quart Dutch oven, heat the oil over medium-high heat, and brown the meat on all sides. Stir the onion and garlic into the browned meat so it is well coated, and turn the heat down to medium. When the onions begin to wilt, add the thyme, basil, rosemary, and white pepper, stirring well to coat everything with the seasonings. Preheat the oven to 300 F.

2 Now add the Marsala, using a wooden spoon or a spatula to stir up all the delicious caramelized bits stuck to the bottom of the pot. Once the Marsala is thoroughly mixed in and is sizzling in the meat juices, add the beef bouillon, rice, and mixed vegetables. Stir to mix well, then bring it back to a slow boil.

3 Carefully transfer the stew pot to the oven. Place on a middle rack, cover the pot tightly, and cook at 300 F for about 4 hours until the meat is tender, the rice is cooked, and the Marsala has worked its magic. ❖

**TIP** If you need more than 4 hours, place the stew in a Crock-Pot in step 2, just before the mixture comes back to a slow boil. Turn on low, and cook 8 hours.

# SMOKY DUCK SOUP

SERVES 2-4

## INGREDIENTS

2 smoked ducks, with some
  meat on

Water to cover ducks

16-ounce can whole kernel
  corn, drained

1½ teaspoons chopped
  (canned) jalapeño peppers

½ to 1 whole raw jalapeño
  pepper (about 3 inches in
  length) minced

John Zent is an avid duck hunter, as well as editor of *American Hunter* magazine. This soup, made from a broth of smoked birds, is proof that he's also an avid and adventurous cook. As with all recipes, adapt this to the smoked ducks you have on hand: John recommends 10 or 12 ducks. But when I went to make it, I had only two smoked ducks in the fridge. (Each had been high-graded, but lots of meat was left.) So for starters, here's a two-duck version of John's soup that can be multiplied to fit your own resources. And, of course, if you want a really meaty soup, save the breast meat of one of those smoked ducks to sweeten the pot.

COOKING

1 In a large pot, break up the birds into three or four pieces and cover with cold water. Bring to a boil, then set on the back burner, on simmer, with the cover slightly ajar. Simmer this way, allowing the steam to escape, for 4-5 hours until you have a potent broth.

2 Remove the duck pieces from the stockpot, and let cool enough to handle. Then pluck the meat from the bones (removing most of the skin) and return the meat to the broth. Add the corn and the canned jalapeño and let the soup come back to a gentle boil. Add the raw, minced jalapeño at the table, and serve with hot cornbread and chilled Mexican beer. ❖

DUCK

&

GOOSE

# WHOLE BIRDS

COOKERY

# RUTH'S SLOW-ROASTED DUCKS

SERVES 8

## INGREDIENTS

4 fat mallards, whole

1 cup Creole seasoning

1 onion, quartered

1 apple, quartered

2 celery stalks

1 green bell pepper, sliced

2 14$^1$/$_2$-ounce cans chicken broth

2 cups water

1 cup cornstarch

While few people share their hunting spots, many are willing to share their favorite duck and goose recipes. The Ruth who shared this recipe with me is the cook at one of the oldest—and most private—hunting lodges out of Stuttgart, Arkansas. How private is it? You can't buy a hunt; you have to be invited. While you're waiting for your invitation in the mail, try out Ruth's favorite recipe. (By the way, these are Ruth's directions, word for word.)

COOKING

1 Shoot, pluck, and clean 4 fat mallards. Preheat oven to 400 F.

2 Season the ducks liberally, inside and out, with Creole seasoning. Place the onion, apple, celery stalks, and green pepper into a covered roasting pan. Pour the chicken broth and water over them. Then place the duck in the roasting pan on top of the fruit and vegetables.

3 Place the roaster, uncovered, in the oven for the first 40 minutes of cooking to brown the ducks. After 40 minutes, cover the roasting pan and continue cooking for 2$^1$/$_2$ hours, until tender.

4 Remove the ducks from the roasting pan and keep warm. Place the pan over a low heat on top of the stove. Add the cornstarch to enough cold water to dissolve it thoroughly, and add it to the pan juices. Cook over low heat, stirring constantly, to thicken the gravy.

5 To serve, debone the breasts, take the legs off the carcass, transfer to serving dish, and pour the gravy over the top. Serve with dirty rice and cornbread. ❖

TIP Ruth uses Tony Cachere's Creole Seasoning, a brand-name seasoning mix. If you can't find it, or a substitute Creole seasoning dry spice mix, Tony's hotline is: 800-551-9066. And yes, it is made in Louisiana, not New York City. But it's available everywhere.

# TRADITIONAL STUFFED DUCKS

SERVES 4

## INGREDIENTS

4 ounces breakfast sausage

$^1/_2$ cup chopped onion

$^1/_2$ cup chopped celery

1 cup chicken bouillon

1 teaspoon dried thyme leaves

$^1/_2$ teaspoon ground sage

$^1/_2$ teaspoon ground black
    pepper

4 cups dried bread cubes

2 tablespoons minced fresh
    parsley

2 mallards

## FOR GRAVY

1$^1/_2$ cups chicken broth

$^1/_4$ teaspoon dried leaf thyme

$^1/_4$ cup milk

$^1/_4$ teaspoon ground black
    pepper

2 teaspoons maple syrup

2 teaspoons cornstarch

2 teaspoons water

The trouble with mallards, usually, is that you hate to make stuffing for just one. But what if you got out your turkey roaster and cooked 2 or even 4 birds side by side? Now that's worth this delicious stuffing—and enough for a holiday feast. This recipe is for 2 mallards; for 4 mallards—or even a goose—allow 1 cup of stuffing per pound of oven-ready bird.

COOKING

1 Break up the sausage in a large skillet and cook over medium heat until lightly browned (about 4-5 minutes). Pour off all but 2 tablespoons of the grease (if necessary).

2 Add the onion and celery to the sausage pan and continue cooking until the celery is bright green and the onion softened (about 4 minutes).

3 Add the bouillon and stir well. Toss the thyme, sage, and pepper into the mixture. When mixed, add the bread cubes and the parsley. Coat the bread cubes well with the sausage mixture. Turn off the heat and let the dressing cool enough so that you can handle it (about 10 minutes).

4 Preheat oven to 350 F. Stuff each bird loosely with the stuffing mixture, and place the birds on a rack, in a shallow roasting pan. Roast, uncovered, about 60 minutes, then raise the heat to 450 F and roast 10 more minutes, until a meat thermometer measures 170 F, for rare to medium-rare. Medium will take another 3-5 minutes.

5 Remove the ducks and the rack from the roaster. Place the roaster on the range top. Let the mallards sit for a few minutes before carving, while you make gravy.

**TIP** The easiest and cheapest way to make lots of dried white or wheat bread cubes for stuffings is to preheat the oven to 200 F. (Cornbread, of course, crumbles without any additional drying.) Then place the bread slices on the racks of your oven. (The average $1^1/_2$-pound loaf has about 18 slices, plus two heels; 5 slices will make 4 cups of cubes. But always dry 1 or 2 slices extra so you don't waste time backtracking if you're short.) Bake for about 20 minutes, then turn the heat off and open the oven door. In 10 minutes the bread slices will be cool enough to handle. Then just cut into 1-inch cubes with a bread or chef's knife.

6 Pour off most of the grease, saving about 2 tablespoons of the pan juices, including the tasty brown bits on the bottom of the pan. Place in a small saucepan, over medium heat. Add the chicken bouillon, thyme, milk, pepper, and maple syrup. In small bowl, dissolve the cornstarch in the 2 teaspoons of cold water. When the pan juices begin to simmer, dribble the cornstarch mixture into the pan. When the sauce thickens into gravy, remove from heat.

7 To serve, remove the stuffing, and place on a platter. Carve the duck, removing the legs first, then slicing the breast. Place that on the platter and spoon the gravy over the top. ❖

---

### STUFFING

You'll need about $1^1/_2$ cups of dressing for each pound of bird, and about 1 cup of bread cubes (or wild rice, white rice, cornbread) for each $1^1/_2$ cups of dressing you want to end up with. Surprisingly, finished dressings usually measure the same as the amount of bread cubes you add to the other ingredients. The above recipe, for instance, uses 4 cups of dried bread cubes and makes 4 cups of finished dressing. Don't ask me where the $^1/_2$ cup of onion, $^1/_2$ cup of celery, 1 cup of bouillon and 4 ounces of sausage went. Stuffing has always been one of those great—and delicious—mysteries of life.

And please remember the usual cautions for any stuffed bird: Don't stuff the bird and let it sit at room temperature for more than 10 minutes. Don't store the leftover stuffing in a cooked bird after you're done eating. Remove stuffing as soon as the bird comes out of the oven, then store any leftovers in a separate container. ■

# SWEET POTATO AND PECAN STUFFED DUCKS

SERVES 4

## INGREDIENTS

3 cups cooked, skinned, and
   diced sweet potatoes

$1/3$ cup minced onion

1 $1/2$ tablespoons minced
   roasted sweet peppers
   (the bottled kind)

2 medium cloves garlic, minced

$1/3$ cup chopped pecans

1 teaspoon salt

$3/8$ teaspoon dried leaf thyme

$3/8$ teaspoon ground white
   pepper

5-7 drops red pepper Tabasco
   sauce

2 mallards (about $1 1/4$ pounds
   each, oven ready)

## SAUCE

Juice of one orange
   (about $1/2$ cup)

2 tablespoons honey

1 tablespoon cornstarch,
   dissolved in $1/4$ cup cold water

There's no reason why a holiday dinner should only highlight the big birds. Maybe you don't like to hunt geese, and have a pile of mallards or pintails in the freezer instead. Why not cook up 2, 4, or even 6 birds to feed the family? They'll be just as good, and with this sweet potato stuffing maybe better than that old standby you've been depending on for years. If you have trouble picking out yams from sweet potatoes, choose the ones with the redder skin. For my money, they have better flavor.

COOKING

1 Preheat the oven to 375 F. In a large bowl, combine the diced sweet potatoes, onion, roasted sweet peppers, garlic, pecans, salt, thyme, white pepper, and Tabasco. Toss to mix.

2 Rinse the ducks and dry inside and out with paper towels. Stuff the bird with the sweet potato mixture. Stuff the neck if you have extra.

3 Place the birds on a rack in a baking pan, and place in the center of the oven. Roast about 60 minutes, until the internal temperature registers about 150 F on a meat thermometer. Then combine the orange juice and honey and pour over the ducks. Return the ducks to the oven and roast another 10-15 minutes, basting often. Remove from the oven and let the ducks stand at room temperature for 5-10 minutes before carving.

4 While the ducks set, pour off the pan juices into a small sauce pan, add the cornstarch and water mixture, and heat until thickened.

5 To serve, transfer sweet potato stuffing to a warm platter. Carve the ducks, and arrange the legs and breast slices across the stuffing. Spoon the sauce over the duck. ❖

# MINCED FRUIT DUCK

**SERVES 4-6**

### INGREDIENTS

6 chopped figs

9 chopped dates

$^{1}/_{2}$ cup coarsely chopped
  unsalted cashews

2 apples, cored and chopped

3 tablespoons cognac, split

Juice and zest of 1 orange, split
  (about 2 teaspoons of zest
  and $^{3}/_{4}$ cup juice)

2 mallards, whole

1 tablespoon cornstarch

Reminiscent of a homemade traditional mincemeat, this stuffing has no bread cubes, rice, or cornbread in it. That makes it incredibly easy to make, and the clay pot always makes wild birds tender and moist. By the way, this fruit stuffing recipe will make a scant 4 cups of dressing, and will work as well for geese—allow $1^{1}/_{2}$ cups dressing per 1 pound of oven-ready bird.

COOKING

1 In a small bowl, combine the figs, dates, cashews, apple, and 1 tablespoon of the cognac. Stir well. Add 2 tablespoons of the freshly squeezed orange juice and stir again. Set aside at room temperature, for at least 1 hour. (This may be prepared the day before and left overnight, tightly covered, in the refrigerator.) Set the clay pot to soak in a sink of cold water to cover the top and bottom. Let soak at least 15 minutes. Dry the ducks inside and out with paper towels.

2 Combine the orange juice and cognac, and set aside.

3 Stuff the mallards with the fruit and nut mixture, loosely. Place in the clay pot and pour $^{1}/_{4}$ cup of the orange juice and cognac mixture over the bird. Place the clay pot in the center of a cold oven.

4 For electric ovens: Turn the oven to 300 F. For gas ovens: Turn the oven to 200 F for 10 minutes; then 250 F for 10 minutes; then 300 F. Roast for 2 hours, leaving the cover off for the last 30 minutes to brown the skin.

**TIP** If you don't own a clay pot, you can also use any small roasting pan with a very tight lid. (Or seal the bird in foil.) Place the duck on a rack in the pan, and pour the orange juice over it. Roast covered at 350 F, for about 1 hour for rare, 10 more minutes for medium. When done, remove the bird from the roasting pan and prepare the sauce in a small saucepan.

5 For gravy: Add the cornstarch to the remaining orange juice and cognac mixture and set it aside to dissolve completely. Pour off as much of the grease as possible, reserving 2 tablespoons of pan juices. Pour that into a saucepan. Heat the pan juices in the saucepan over medium heat, and add the orange juice and cornstarch mixture. Stir into the pan juices until well mixed, and simmer until the pan juices thicken, about 4-5 minutes.

6 To serve, arrange the ducks on a platter, whole. Spoon the orange and cognac sauce over the top for a festive presentation. Then carve at the table. Serve with sweet potatoes, creamed onions, and fresh green beans. ❖

---

### HOW DO YOU KNOW WHEN THE BIRD IS DONE?

Don't cook the goose, or any waterfowl, until the juices run clear. Unlike chicken and turkeys, waterfowl juices NEVER RUN CLEAR. There will always be a little red tint, no matter how well done the birds are.

A meat thermometer is the best way to judge when your dinner is ready. All you need to decide is how done is done, then refer to the readings for rare, medium, and medium-well for the commercial birds. Commercially raised birds, with all that extra fat, can afford to be cooked to well-done, and probably are safer to eat that way. However, for our lower-fat wild birds, this is a recipe for dry meat. When dry roasting, the tastiest, juiciest wild game eating will always be on the rare side of well-done. ■

# WILD RICE STUFFED MALLARDS

**SERVES 4-6**

## INGREDIENTS

2 tablespoons butter

3 cups cooked wild rice

1$^1/_2$ cups coarsely chopped walnuts

$^2/_3$ cup medium-dry sherry

$^3/_4$ cup chicken bouillon

1 bay leaf

$^1/_4$ teaspoon ground black pepper

2 strips bacon

2 mallards

## COOKING

1 In a skillet, melt the butter over medium heat and add the rice and walnuts. Sauté until the pan is pretty dry, then add the sherry, bouillon, bay leaf, and pepper. Turn the heat down to a simmer, and let that mixture cook until the bottom of the pan is pretty dry when you stir the rice.

2 Remove the bay leaf from the stuffing and discard it. Loosely stuff the ducks with the rice mixture. Cut each slice of bacon in half, and drape 2 halves across each duck. Place the ducks on a rack in a shallow roasting pan and roast 60 minutes at 350 F, then raise the temperature for the last 10 minutes to 450 F, to crisp the skin. A meat thermometer should register 170 F, or medium-done after this.

3 To serve, remove stuffing and carve the mallards. ❖

**TIP** To make 2 cups of perfect wild rice, bring 2 cups of water to a boil and add 1 cup of wild rice to the pot. Stir, and cover the pot. When the water comes back to a boil, stir the rice again, then cover and reduce the heat to a low simmer. The rice should take 15-20 minutes. Taste it when all the water is absorbed. Older rice can take more water to make it tender. If your rice is still crunchy, add another $^1/_4$ cup of water and continue cooking on very low heat another 5 minutes, or until all the water is gone.

# ROTISSERIE DUCK

SERVES 2

## INGREDIENTS

1/4 cup bottled Del Monte chili
    sauce
1 tablespoon honey
1 teaspoon Worcestershire
    sauce
1 whole mallard
1 cup mesquite chips

Here's another way to cook duck indirectly—by spit roasting it—to avoid all the fat fires on the barbecue. If your barbecue doesn't have a rotisserie unit, you can add a "universal" electric spit for under $30. The result is a moist, tender, and quick duck that will please anybody.

PREPARATION

1 Prepare a drip pan: Take two 20-inch lengths of 12-inch-wide aluminum foil and lay one on top of the other. Now fold up the sides and ends about 2 inches and fold the corners over. Remove the cooking grate of the barbecue and lay this drip pan in the middle of the fire rack, over the coals.

2 Preheat the barbecue to about 375 F, or medium heat.

COOKING

1 In a small bowl, combine the chili sauce, honey, and Worcestershire sauce. (Melt the honey in a microwave for 10 seconds on high (700 watts) if it's crystallized.) Rinse and dry the duck thoroughly, and attach it securely to the spit.

2 Once the barbecue is at 375 F or medium heat, place the spitted duck on the barbecue, start it rotating, and spread the mesquite chips over the hot coals (or lava rocks, as in a propane barbecue).

3 Roast for about 25 minutes, to medium or medium-rare, spooning sauce over the duck 2-3 times while it cooks. Check with a meat thermometer to be sure the duck is done to your taste—about 160 F for medium, 170 F for medium-well. ❖

# BARBECUED GOOSE WITH CUMBERLAND SAUCE

SERVES 4

---

INGREDIENTS

1 whole goose, about 6 pounds

1 whole orange, peeled

8x12x1 inch disposable
    aluminum drip pan

2 tablespoons butter

3 tablespoons dry red wine

1 teaspoon Worcestershire
    sauce

$^1/_4$ cup red currant jelly

---

Cumberland sauce is one of the most traditional game sauces of the British Isles. But it does double duty in our house. In the dog days of August, we'll cook this dish on the barbecue to keep from heating up the house. And when Thanksgiving is kind to us, barbecuing the main course of our holiday feast leaves lots of room for pies and creamed onions in the kitchen oven. Either way, this is an easy-to-cook meal that looks fabulous at the table.

COOKING

1 Preheat barbecue to 350 F, for indirect cooking (see sidebar on page 62).

2 Rinse the goose in cold water; pat dry with paper towels inside and out. Place the peeled orange inside the goose.

3 Set the goose in the drip pan. Close the barbecue and cook until the meat thermometer reads 140-150 F (about 10 minutes per pound for about 6 pounds of bird in summer; longer on cool days). You'll get a slightly pink bird. Place the goose on a platter to cool. Remove the orange and save to make the sauce.

4 In a small skillet, melt the butter over medium heat. Trim the dark brown crust from the orange, and dice the rest, adding it to the melted butter. Sauté 2-3 minutes, until you smell the orange, then add the wine, Worcestershire, and currant jelly. Once the jelly has melted, lower heat to simmer. Cook another 10 minutes, until the sauce thickens. Serve the goose hot with hot Cumberland Sauce. Or serve both chilled. ❖

# DEEP-FRIED WHOLE CANADA GOOSE

SERVES 6-8

## INGREDIENTS

1 whole goose
1 whole orange, peeled
1 whole apple, peeled
1 whole onion, peeled
1 teaspoon salt
1 teaspoon pepper
Peanut or canola oil to cover

Goose always too dry? There are two answers. One is to cook it rare to medium-rare. The other? Fry it. Frying not only seals in all the natural juices, it actually adds a few ounces of its own humidity to the dinner plate. This is another outdoor dish, best done with a regular "turkey" fryer and set up off the beaten track. Why? The turkey fryer comes complete with a bird lifter and a safety rail for the pot, but it is hot oil, which takes a while to heat and cool down. As with all game meats, don't overcook the bird: about $3^1/_2$ minutes per pound is recommended. For this Canada, which weighed 6 pounds, I allowed 18 minutes. Adjust your timing to the weight of your goose, then before you turn the cooker off, check the bird with a meat thermometer to see that it's done enough for your tastes.

### PREPARATION

1 To see how much oil you'll need to fry the bird, place bird on the carrier and lower into the pot. Add cold water, until the goose is completely covered. Now lift the goose out and measure the water. That's how much oil you'll need. (In my pot, which is 12 inches diameter, this 6-pound goose took 6 gallons to cover. At 6 gallons, canola oil is a lot cheaper than peanut oil and has almost as high a smoking point. So unless you're planning to fry hundreds of geese, or you're Bill Gates, use canola.)

2 Now give that goose the twice over. Is it completely, absolutely, totally thawed? Even a small amount of frost inside will make the oil spatter more. So be sure. Give it a quick zap in the microwave (see proper thawing, pages 155-156). Or just delay the frying until the bird has no ice crystals inside or out.

**3** Set up the turkey fryer outdoors, fill with the proper amount of oil, and cover with lid. Light the burner. When the long-legged turkey-frying thermometer registers 350 F, you're ready to cook.

### COOKING

**1** Dry the goose inside and out with paper towels. Halve the orange, apple, and onion and place inside the body cavity. Rub the salt and pepper on the outside of the bird. Place the goose on the frying rack, legs up.

**2** At 350 F, lower the goose slowly into the hot oil, without splashing. Wear the longest oven mitts you've got, and use the lifting hook provided with the fryer to keep arms and hands out of harm's way. (And wear long pants, not shorts. Even the best-dried bird will spatter a bit when it hits the hot oil.) Leave the lid off once the goose is in the oil.

**3** Allow $3^1/_2$ minutes per pound of bird; set a timer, then remove the turkey and place on paper towel–lined pan. It is done when the internal temperature registers about 160-170 F on a meat thermometer. The legs will be quite loose if the bird is done as well.

**4** Let the bird cool 10 minutes, then carve as you would a Christmas goose. Serve with other summertime treats, like coleslaw, potato salad, and ice-cold watermelon slices for dessert. ❖

# CLAY-POT GOOSE WITH PINEAPPLE-MAPLE SAUCE

SERVES 3-4

## INGREDIENTS

1 snow goose,
  about 1¹/₂-2 pounds
2 tablespoons unsweetened
  pineapple juice
2 tablespoons maple syrup
1 teaspoon spicy brown mustard

This particular recipe is one we developed for less-than-perfect-tasting birds, but the clay pot can just as easily be used to cook mild-flavored mallards and Canadas to perfection. It's important to follow the manufacturer's directions. I know from experience. Our first clay pot died in a spectacular flood when we broke rule #1. We placed it, wet, in a preheated oven. Undaunted, and addicted to moist birds, we immediately bought a replacement. You'll know why when you try this recipe.

PREPARATION

1 Do not preheat oven.
2 Place the clay pot in a sink full of cold water to cover the top and bottom. Let soak for at least 15 minutes. Take one more look at the goose, trimming rough edges and pulling feathers you missed last fall. Dry inside and out with paper towels.

## CLAY POTS: THE OLDEST NEW FAD FOR BIRD HUNTERS

If you cook a lot of birds, like them more than medium-rare, and don't like them dry, you really should try a clay pot. They infuse moisture into all wild birds—upland as well as waterfowl—and allow you to cook them to higher internal temperatures without losing as much moisture. A lot like a water smoker, but without the smoke—and you're cooking indoors. An advantage during the holiday season.

I've included a recipe each for both ducks (see page 42) and geese, using a clay pot; one recipe browns the outside of the bird and one does not. Feel free to substitute cooking methods on any whole-bird recipe. ∎

COOKING

**1** Combine the pineapple juice, maple syrup, and mustard in a small bowl. Microwave 10-12 seconds on high (700 watts) to liquefy the syrup. Stir the mixture well.

**2** Place the goose in the clay pot, breast up, and pour the juice mixture slowly over the breast, legs, and wings. Cover the pot and place in the center of a cold oven.

**3** For electric ovens: Turn the oven to 300 F. For gas ovens: Turn the oven to 200 F for 10 minutes; then 250 F for ten minutes, then 300 F. Roast for 2 hours.

**4** Remove the goose from the pot and carve as you would a Christmas goose. Serve with pan juices. (If you like lots of sauce, heat up some more of the pineapple, mustard, and maple syrup concoction in a saucepan just before the goose is done. Then combine that and the pan juices together to serve at the table.) ❖

## CORNBREAD

Make your own cornbread, or use this quick recipe.

**Yields 5 cups of crumbs**

**INGREDIENTS**
³/₄ **cups white flour**
**3 teaspoons baking powder**
**1 tablespoon sugar**
**1¹/₄ cup yellow corn meal**
**1 egg, beaten**
**2 tablespoons melted butter or**
   **margarine**
**1 cup milk**

COOKING
1. Preheat the oven to 425 F. Grease an 8x8 inch pan.
2. Combine the flour, baking powder, and sugar and sift into a large bowl. In a separate bowl, combine the egg, butter, and milk. Stir to combine the liquids, then add to the dry ingredients. Stir the batter just enough to moisten the dry ingredients and spoon into the baking pan. Bake 20-25 minutes until golden brown. Cool, then crumble 2 cups of the loaf, slightly less than half of the bread, for the dressing. Serve the leftover cornbread with your dinner. ∎

# SOUTH-OF-THE-BORDER STUFFED GOOSE

SERVES 6-8

## INGREDIENTS

6 ounces chorizo sausage

1 cup chopped onion

$1/2$ cup chopped celery

3 cups crumbled cornbread

$1/2$ teaspoon ground cumin

$1/2$ teaspoon dried leaf oregano

$1/4$ teaspoon chili powder

$1/2$ teaspoon salt

$1/2$ teaspoon ground black
   pepper

1 cup chicken bouillon

$1/2$ cup chopped fresh cilantro

1 goose
   (2-3 pounds oven-ready)

For those who like their birds whole and roasted for special (or even not-so-special) occasions, but are looking for a little different flavor, this is the way to go. Cornbread is a juicy, delicious way to make dressing taste special. Use this recipe or your own favorite. Either way, an 8x8 inch pan of cornbread breaks up into about 5 cups of crumbs. Enough for the bird, and a little to tide you over till dinner, too. Look for fresh cilantro next to the parsley.

COOKING

1 In a large skillet, over medium heat, sauté the chorizo until it is no longer pink. Drain off all but 2 tablespoons of the grease. Toss the onion and celery into the browned sausage and continue sautéing until the vegetables are soft, about 6-8 minutes.

2 In a large bowl, break up the cornbread and add the cumin, oregano, chili powder, salt, and pepper. Toss this into the skillet with the bouillon until the cornbread has absorbed all the liquid, about 2 minutes. Remove from heat and add the cilantro.

3 Preheat the oven to 325 F. Stuff the goose loosely. Place any leftover stuffing in a baking dish and refrigerate. (Bake it later, for 60 minutes.)

4 Place the goose, breast up, on a rack in a roasting pan. Cover the roasting pan tightly and place in the 325 F oven. Roast about 15-20 minutes per pound of bird (weigh the bird before stuffing), allowing the bird to brown with the lid off for the last half hour of cooking. A medium-rare bird will be about 150 F on the meat thermometer, sitting fresh out of the oven. (The thermometer will rise another 7-10 degrees within 10 minutes of removing it from the oven.) A medium bird will register about 160 F. For the 3-pound bird in these directions, allow 45 minutes with the cover on, then another 20 minutes with it off for medium done. ❖

# TRADITIONAL HOLIDAY STUFFED GOOSE WITH LINGONBERRY SAUCE

SERVES 6-8

## INGREDIENTS

4 ounces breakfast sausage
1 apple, diced
1 cup onion, diced
2 stalks celery, diced
3 teaspoons herbes de Provence,
  crushed, divided
$1/3$ cup apple cider
2 teaspoons chicken bouillon
  granules dissolved in 1 cup
  hot water
6 cups dried bread cubes
Whole Canada goose,
  4-5 pounds, oven-ready
$1/4$ pound (1 cube) butter, melted
$1/2$ teaspoon salt
$1/4$ teaspoon ground pepper
$1^1/2$ teaspoons orange zest

## LINGONBERRY SAUCE

$3/4$ cup water
$1/2$ cup chicken bouillon
$1/3$ cup lingonberry preserves
2 tablespoons sour cream
1 tablespoon cornstarch

Predicting how much stuffing you'll need for a goose is almost as hard as predicting how many geese will fly over your blind. Geese come in all different sizes, but if you allow about $1^1/2$ cups of dressing for each pound of oven-ready bird, you'll have enough. This recipe will fill a 4-5 pound goose loosely, as recommended. As for the lingonberries, they're a tart, round fruit a lot like a cranberry. If you can't find lingonberry preserves, substitute whole cranberry sauce.

### PREPARATION

1 Preheat the oven to 325 F.

2 In a large skillet, break up the sausage and sauté over medium heat until no pink remains. Pour off all but 1 tablespoon of the fat. Add the chopped apple, onion, celery, and only 2 teaspoons of the herbes de Provence mixture. Stir well, and continue sautéing until the apples and onions are soft, about 6-8 minutes. Add the apple cider (the better the cider, the better the dressing) and let it soak into the vegetables; sauté about 3-4 minutes. Toss the bread cubes into the sausage mixture. Then sprinkle the chicken bouillon over the stuffing, until all the bread is moistened.

### COOKING

1 Check the goose for stray feathers, and trim raw edges. Then dry inside and out with paper towels. Stuff the body cavity loosely with the stuffing. Tuck the legs in and tie tightly together with a string, so they rest against the body cavity.

2 Place the stuffed goose in an aluminum-foil-lined baking pan. In a small saucepan, melt the butter and add the rest of the herbes de Provence, salt, pepper, and orange zest. Cut 2 pieces of cheese-

Have you ever added orange juice to a recipe and found it rather blah in flavor? Well, that's because the most intense flavor of an orange (or lemon, the two most commonly "zested" fruits) is in that microscopically thin layer of color on the OUTSIDE of the fruit. The trick, however, is to remove the color without getting any of the less-than-palatable white pulp just a millimeter below.

There is a cheap little tool called a zester, available at any serious kitchen store, which makes the job incredibly easy. Or you can use a common potato peeler. Just use a light touch—imagine you're shaving a soft-boiled egg—and then mince the peels before adding them to the recipe. Oh, one more thing. In recipes where you both zest and juice the orange or lemon, it is infinitely easier if you zest first, then juice. ■

cloth long enough and wide enough to cover the bird, and sop up the all the herbed butter with the cheesecloth. Lay it across the breast, legs, and wings.

3 Close the foil over the bird and seal tightly. Place in the center of the oven and cook about 20 minutes per pound, including a 30-minute period to brown with the lid off. For this 4-5 pound bird, allow 80-100 minutes to cook with the foil and cheesecloth on, then another 30 minutes with the breast bare, at 400 F so it browns. Reserve the cheesecloth for the gravy, soaking it in a bowl with $1/2$ cup of the water. (The trade-off here is for moisture. So while this won't be the best browned bird you ever saw, it will be the most moist.)

4 Test with a meat thermometer when your time is up: it should read about 135 F before you begin to brown it. (The bird will increase to about 170 F with the browning, while still staying moist and delicious. Then the bird—and thermometer—will rise another 7-10 degrees to about 180 F in the first 10 minutes out of the oven. (And don't worry about the bird being too tough cooked to that temperature. Those two layers of cheesecloth will keep the bird quite tender.)

5 To make the gravy: Wring the water-soaked cheesecloth into a saucepan. Add the bouillon, lingonbery preserves, and sour cream. When it comes to a slow boil, add the cornstarch (dissolved in the last $1/4$ cup of cold water) to the sauce. Stir until thickened.

To serve, remove the stuffing and transfer it to a warm bowl. Carve the bird and arrange on a warm serving platter with buttered carrots, Brussels sprouts, and the lingonberry sauce spooned over the thinly sliced meat. ❖

## DRY ROASTING WATERFOWL: IS IT THE BEST WAY TO COOK THEM?

There's something magical about serving a whole-roasted duck or goose at the table. For one thing, it's an incredible investment in time and energy. Over the course of hunting season, you've looked for the perfect bird—a fat, healthy young bird, with perfect skin that would look great on the table. Then you spent the time to pluck it carefully, diligently pulling all the pin feathers and searing the strays your hands couldn't grab. That bird took up valuable freezer space, maybe even forced you to buy a new freezer. And now is the moment of truth, when you cook that beautiful bird and serve it to hunters and non-hunters alike.

Actually, maybe the word I'm looking for isn't magical. Maybe it's stressful. Or nerve-racking. Especially if you've never done it before.

**Just remember 3 things:**
1. **This is a wild animal. There isn't a lot of fat.**
2. **This is a wild animal. There isn't a lot of fat.**
3. **This is a wild animal. There isn't a lot of fat.**

Once you have those three things in mind, remember that the chief complaint about wild birds is that they're too dry, and the chief cooking advice most people get is to cook the heck out of them because they have cooties. As my Mom used to say, "You don't know where they've been."

Well, the truth is wild animals have no more cooties than commercially raised ones, and maybe even fewer because they don't live in such close quarters. And if you cook wild birds to the consistency of a hockey puck, they will be dry.

Here's what you do: Go out and buy yourself a $4 meat thermometer. Then cook one small bird whole, say on the rotisserie, until it registers 150 F on the thermometer. (It will rise to about 160 F in the first few minutes after you remove it from the heat. Trust me.) Let it sit about 10 minutes at room temperature. Then slice off a piece of the breast and eat it.

If you still don't like medium-rare birds after that, make a point to avoid cooking any dry-roasted whole birds in this section. If you cook dry-roasted birds until all the pink is out of them, they will be dry and tough. Choose Ruth's Slow-Roasted Ducks, Deep-Fried Whole Canada Goose, the Clay-Pot Goose with Pineapple-Maple Sauce, or the Traditional Holiday Stuffed Goose. In other words, any recipe that cooks the bird long and slow or covered and moist. Then you can cook the bird to 185 F, or well-done, and still enjoy a moist, tender holiday meal.

Those recipes are also good for first-time cooks because they don't need to be timed as closely.

One more thing. When I was a kid, we went to my grandmother's house for holiday dinners. She would always buy a 25- or 30-pound turkey, start it at the crack of dawn, and serve dinner around 3 in the afternoon. It's taken me years to break that habit, even with commercial turkeys. Put a Canada goose in the oven at dawn, and you'll be eating dinner midmorning. Or hockey pucks at 3.

Dry roasting is a great way to cook waterfowl, but take it easy. Sleep in. Even a 10-pound goose will only take about 20 minutes per pound stuffed, 15 unstuffed. That's dinner in less than 3 hours. You can use the extra time to go hunting. ■

PS: All bird weights given in these recipes are for oven-ready birds. That weight is about $1/2$ the weight of the bird on the wing, and will provide about 50 percent of that weight in edible meat. So an 8-pound goose on the wing (4 pounds plucked and drawn), will provide about 2 pounds of boned meat. Allowing 4 ounces per serving, that's about 8 servings. The same ratio works for smaller birds.

# BEST-DRESSED GOOSE

SERVES 2-4

## INGREDIENTS

¼ pound bacon

1 cup chopped onion

1 cup chopped celery

1 teaspoon dry mustard

2 teaspoon dried leaf thyme

1 teaspoon dried leaf sage

1 teaspoon black pepper

4 cups dried bread cubes

3 cups brut champagne, in all

2 eggs, lightly beaten

1 goose, 4-5 pounds

1 tablespoon flour

¼ cup sweet hot mustard

1 tablespoon prepared creamy
   horseradish

## COOKING

**1** Ahead: Cook the bacon until crisp. Place the strips on paper towels to drain, and reserve the pan drippings. When the bacon strips are cool enough to handle, break them up into 1-inch pieces.

**2** In a large skillet, melt 2 tablespoons of the bacon drippings over medium heat. Sauté the onion and celery in the drippings until tender. Stir in the mustard, thyme, sage, and black pepper and mix well. Then add this onion mixture to the bread cubes.

**3** In a small bowl, combine the two cups of champagne with the eggs. Drizzle over the bread cubes. Toss lightly to coat all the dry bread. Stir in the bacon pieces.

**4** Cut a piece of cheesecloth that will cover the breast and legs of the goose. Melt 3 tablespoons of the bacon grease, and soak the cheesecloth in it. Preheat the oven to 325 F.

**5** Stuff the goose loosely with the bread mixture, and place breast up on a rack in a shallow roasting pan. Cover the breast and legs with the bacon-coated cheesecloth. Roast covered about 20-25 minutes per pound, checking the internal temperature with a meat thermometer about 30 minutes before you think it will be done. Rare will be around 165 F, medium 175 F.

**6** Remove the dressing and cover to keep warm. Allow the goose to sit 10 minutes before carving. Start the gravy. Pour off the grease, then heat the pan juices on the stove top over medium heat. Combine the flour with the last cup of champagne. Stir gently. Add this mixture and the sweet-hot mustard slowly to the pan, stirring continuously. When the mixture thickens, remove from heat and add the horseradish. ❖

DUCK

&

GOOSE

# PARTING IT OUT
## BREASTS, LEGS, & TRIMMINGS

COOKERY

# MARINATED DUCK BREASTS

**SERVES 4**

### INGREDIENTS

³/₄ cup soy sauce
1 teaspoon ground ginger
¹/₄ teaspoon garlic powder
¹/₄ cup vegetable oil
Breasts of 2 mallards, skinned

This may be the most popular recipe in duck cookery. I've used it for years, and no matter where I hunt waterfowl, someone will mention this recipe in some form—usually some variation of Great Uncle Bubba's Magic Duck Elixir. Try a prepared soy sauce and ginger marinade, or use this from scratch. Then the only trick is to cook the breast hot and quick, leaving as much pink (or red) as your family will allow. But remember, the more you cook them, the tougher—and dryer—wild birds get. If that's your main complaint about duck and goose, give pink a try.

### PREPARATION

**1** In a resealable plastic bag or non-corrosive bowl, combine the soy sauce, ginger, garlic powder, and oil. Shake or stir to dissolve everything.

**2** Trim the duck breasts, and dry each one with paper towels. Place them in the marinade for 30-40 minutes.

### COOKING

**1** Prepare your barbecue for hot cooking. Preheat a propane barbecue for 10 minutes, then turn down to medium-high. Or start 40 charcoal briquettes, wait 25 minutes. (Adjust the propane controls or the charcoal grill vents to fine-tune the cooking temperature. Open vents and close up the briquette pile to increase heat; close down vents and spread pile to decrease heat.)

**2** Drain the breasts from the marinade, pat dry, and place on the hot grill. Cook about 4 minutes a side for rare mallards; 5-6 minutes

*Very Good, but ^ can taste rather salty if not dried with paper towel before putting on grill*

for medium. (This time is for breasts taken from 2-3 pound ducks, about 1-inch thick. For larger ducks, with thicker breasts, allow a little more time, but beware of overcooking them.

**3** Slice thin, across the grain, and serve on a warm platter with potato salad. ❖

Patting cubes and slices of meat or whole breasts and legs down with paper towels before cooking may sound silly, but there are two basic reasons why you do it.

You'll most often find this direction in recipes where you need to brown meat in preheated oil, and hot oil and water don't mix well. So the first advantage of drying is that you don't get burned.

But the drying also helps with the flavor of a dish. Have you ever noticed a gray liquid bubbling up in the frying pan when you are browning meat? That gray liquid is diluting your spices. Drying the meat with a paper towel before cooking eliminates the gray liquid. Properly browned meat will leave the pan a rich brown color, not a steamed gray.

Now, if you dried the meat and still get some of that gray liquid, push the meat to one side of the pan, then tip the pan a few degrees away from the meat—carefully—and dab up the extra liquid with a paper towel. You could also lightly flour the meat to prevent oil-water splatters, but that would change the sauce. Paper towels don't. For best effect, set the meat on a couple of layers of paper towels, and cover with 1 more layer. Press to dry, and let the meat sit sandwiched there for a few minutes, while you prepare the pan. ∎

# CARIBOU CAMP GOOSE BREASTS

**SERVES 4-6**

### INGREDIENTS

**8 ounces Tang (prepared
    according to pkg. directions)
8 ounces lemon Crystal Light
    (ditto)
1 medium yellow onion,
    chopped
Breasts of 2 snow geese**

L ast August, my husband, John, was in caribou camp and succeed-ed in acquiring the McNab Grand Slam. In one day: a caribou bull, a couple of nice Arctic char, a brace of snow geese, and a nap. Now, the caribou was a trophy, the char put on ice, and the nap as ephemeral as a summer's day. But the snow geese were lunch. Problem was how to prepare them in a camp heavy on peanut butter and white bread and light on haute (or even medium-haute) cuisine. His efforts received the ultimate of compliments: the geese were enjoyed by all. Here is his recipe.

### COOKING

**1** In a saucepan, combine the Tang, Crystal Light, and chopped onion. Bring to a boil, lower heat to simmer, and let cook about 5-7 minutes. Remove from heat and let cool to "room" temperature.

**2** Skin and dry the goose breasts. When the Tang mixture is cool, pour it into a large bowl, over the goose breasts. Let marinate for 30-45 minutes.

**3** Prepare a grill or open fire for cooking on high heat.

**4** Lightly oil the cooking grate to prevent sticking. Place the goose breasts on the grate and grill about 4 minutes a side for medium-rare. No more than 5 minutes a side for medium. (Note that the cooking time is about the same as for the mallards in the previous recipe.) Slice acoss the grain and serve as an appetizer while the cook makes dinner, or as a main course with your camp dinner. ❖

# BUTTERFLIED GOOSE BREASTS

SERVES 2-4

INGREDIENTS

**1 snow goose breast**
**¹/₄ cup brown sugar**

Here's another recipe found in a goose blind, and one of the easiest I've ever cooked. The only secret to this one is a sharp knife, to make the butterflying easier. And the only secret to the butterfly method is to not cut totally through the breast. More flavor, less thickness, less cooking time. And a delicious result. You can't ask for more from a goose blind.

COOKING

**1** Bone and skin the breast off the goose carcass. Place each side on a cutting board and, with a sharp fillet or boning knife parallel to the cutting board, slice the meat almost in half—in thickness. Leave about an inch attached. Open the breast at the cut, and press it out on the cutting board.

**2** Dry with paper towels, on both sides. Lightly oil the grill rack on your barbecue and preheat. You'll want high heat for the cooking.

**3** When the fire is ready, place both pieces of the butterflied breast cut-side down on the grill and rub 2 tablespoons of brown sugar into the top of each. Grill about 3 minutes on first side, 1 on second side for medium-rare. Slice across the grain, and serve with potato salad and bread-and-butter pickles. ❖

To butterfly the breast, lay it flat on a cutting board, and, with your knife parallel to the board, slice the thickness in half: leave an inch on the far side uncut, so you can then turn the breast over, press it down with your palm, and have a single, double-wide piece of fast-grilling goose.

# GRILLED JALAPEÑO BREASTS

**SERVES 3-4**

*Split one breast for 2 people*

## INGREDIENTS

**Breast of young goose, boned out**

**1 clove garlic, minced**

**¼ cup soy sauce**

**2 tablespoons bacon drippings**

**1 teaspoon pickled jalapeño juice**

**2 pickled jalapeño peppers**

*Very good! Quick — can be broiled*

This is one of the reasons I love propane barbecues. Not only is this a delicious way to cook goose breasts on a hot summer's day, but in the winter, when you need a bit of a pick me up, you can run outside and light that propane grill and know it will be ready to cook in 10 minutes. No fuss, no muss. No failures. And the marinade takes only 30-45 minutes.

## COOKING

1 Place the goose breast halves in a shallow dish. Rub the garlic over the tops and pour the soy sauce over all. Let sit for 30-45 minutes. Heat the bacon drippings and combine with pickled pepper juice.

2 Preheat the grill to medium heat. Pour off marinade, and make a small slit in the side of each section of breast. Insert the jalapeño pepper. Grill about 7-8 minutes a side, brushing with the bacon drippings and jalapeño juice mixture. Slice across the grain and serve hot. ❖

---

### BEATING THE FAT FIRES

Used to be that barbecuing a duck or goose meant standing guard with fully loaded water pistols to prevent fat fires from ruining dinner. I've got nothing against water pistols, but when suppertime is getting close, I've got a lot better things to do with my time. Enter indirect cooking.

If you have a propane barbecue, you need two burners, with only one lit. With a charcoal unit, simply build the fire on one side of the fire grate. Preheat both to 350 F. Then place the goose on a cast-iron poultry grate over an aluminum drip pan, and place both on the side where the fire isn't.

The goose drips into the pan, not the fire, so there's no flare-up to douse, and barbecuing the goose outdoors is a great way to beat the summer heat. It's also a delicious way to cook any waterfowl.

We'll just have to use those water pistols for direct cooking. ■

# INSIDE-OUT STUFFED GOOSE

SERVES 4-6

## INGREDIENTS

1 orange, peeled and chopped
   in large chunks
1 apple, peeled, cored, and
   chopped in large chunks
1 medium onion, chopped
Breast of one goose, boned,
   skinned, and towel dried
1 package Stove Top stuffing,
   chicken flavored
$1^2/_3$ cups water
1 tablespoon butter

My neighbor Kathleen Jepson hates dry goose. So she borrowed this recipe (almost) from a friend and has used it for years. The almost? Kathleen makes her own dressing, instead of the ready-to-eat variety, but the goose is still moist, and the box shortcut takes a lot less time and trouble. If you want to follow Kathleen's lead, make up 3 cups of your own favorite dressing and use it instead of Stove Top convenience.

### COOKING

1 In a pot just large enough to fit the breast meat in a single layer, toss the orange, apple, and onion chunks. Nestle the goose breast into this mixture. Add enough cold water to just cover the meat.

2 Bring the pot to a boil, reduce the heat to low, and cover. Simmer until tender, about 90 minutes.

3 Toss the Stove Top ingredients in the $1^2/_3$ cups of water and set aside for 10 minutes. Preheat the oven to 350 F, and spread the butter in the bottom of an 8- or 9-inch-square baking pan.

4 When the breast meat is tender, remove the meat and discard the cooking mixture. Set the breast in the baking dish and cover with the stuffing. Bake until the dressing is cooked, about 30 minutes. Serve hot, with buttered Brussels sprouts. ❖

# HARVEST DINNER

**SERVES 4**

### INGREDIENTS

1 pound breast meat, (dabbler
   duck or good-tasting goose)
2 tablespoons canola or olive oil
1 medium yellow onion,
   sliced thin
2 cloves garlic, minced
1 cup thinly sliced zucchini
3 cups coarsely chopped
   ripe tomatoes
1 cup fresh corn,
   cut off the cob
1 tablespoon minced fresh basil
   leaves (1 teaspoon dried leaf)
$1/2$ teaspoon salt
$1/2$ teaspoon pepper
$1/4$ cup grated Parmesan cheese

One of our favorite things to do in the late summer/early fall is to make a few meals whose ingredients are mainly from our hunting and gardening efforts. The temptation is to plant with a recipe in mind, but Mother Nature is not always predictable. Some summers are so cool that the harvest meal is a root stew: rutabagas, carrots, onions, and turnips paired with caribou. But this summer was warm—a bumper crop of tomatoes, onions, and corn—even the herb corner did well. The harvest dinner was quite delicious.

### COOKING

1 Cut up the breast meat into 1-inch cubes and dry with paper towels.

2 Heat the oil in a large skillet, over medium heat. Add the onion, garlic, and zucchini slices to the pan and sauté until they begin to brown lightly (about 3-4 minutes). Add the tomatoes, cubed breast meat, basil, salt, and pepper and continue sautéing over medium heat, until the meat is cooked through (about 15 minutes).

3 Serve over spaghetti, with Parmesan cheese. ❖

**TIP** Commercially grown tomatoes (as well as other vegetables) can be substituted, of course, but choose ones that are prime. Zucchini should be small and slender, the onion skins shiny and unbroken, and the tomatoes, if not completely ripe, can be finished off indoors on a sunny windowsill.

# TEN-MINUTE TEAL

SERVES 2-3

## INGREDIENTS

Breasts of 3 teal

$^1/_2$ cup chicken broth

$^1/_8$ cup soy sauce

1 teaspoon ground ginger

3 tablespoons fresh
   orange juice

2$^1/_2$ tablespoons chopped
   salted peanuts

2 tablespoons butter

$^1/_3$ cup thinly sliced celery

$^1/_2$ cup onion, diced

$^2/_3$ cup thinly sliced carrots

3 cups cooked rice

As much as I love big meals with gravies, sauces, and delicious side dishes, most nights I'm way too tired and stressed out to cook anything that takes more than 20 minutes of my time. This is one of those dishes. And the best thing is that the intense, tangy combination of soy sauce and salted peanuts makes this a dish that doesn't compromise one iota on flavor.

COOKING

1 Rinse the teal breasts and dry well with paper towels. In a small bowl, combine the broth, soy sauce, ginger, orange juice, and peanuts. Stir, and set aside.

2 In a 10-inch skillet, melt the butter over medium-high heat. Add the celery, onion, and carrot. Reduce the heat to medium. Gently sauté the vegetables until tender, about 5 minutes.

3 Add the soy sauce mixture to the pan, bring to a gentle boil over medium-high heat, then reduce to simmer. Wipe each breast in the sauce, and nestle into the pan juices. Cover and cook 10 minutes. Serve over rice. ❖

# DUCK IN PLUM SAUCE

**SERVES 2**

## INGREDIENTS

2 large, ripe purple plums

1 tablespoon canola oil

Breast of 1 mallard, about
    8 ounces

1 tablespoon butter

1 tablespoon apricot jam

1 tablespoon hot water

1/4 teaspoon pepper

1 tablespoon fresh lime juice

This is one of my favorite quick dishes for dabbler duck breasts. If you want to substitute a delicious Canada goose just check the weight: a mallard breast weighs about 8 ounces. A Canada is about double that—so you need to double the rest of the recipe to have lots of sauce.

### COOKING

1 Preheat the oven to 250 F. Slice the plums (about 1 cup). Set aside.

2 In an 8-inch oven-proof skillet, heat the oil to the smoking point (medium-high), sear the duck breast, about 2-3 minutes to a side. Place skillet in center of the oven to finish cooking (5 minutes for medium-rare). Start sauce.

3 Melt butter over medium heat in second skillet. Add the plums. Sauté about 4 minutes until soft. Add the jam, water, and pepper. Stir until the jam liquefies, turn off the heat, and stir in lime juice. Slice the breast across the grain, place on a bed of wild rice, and spoon sauce over top. ❖

# PINTAIL PICCATA

SERVES 2

## INGREDIENTS

Breast of 1 pintail duck

1 cup buttermilk

$1/2$ teaspoon salt

$1/4$ teaspoon pepper

2 tablespoons flour

2 tablespoons butter

2 tablespoons olive oil

1 clove garlic, minced

Juice of 1 lemon

$1/2$ cup white wine

1 tablespoon whole drained
   capers

2 tablespoons grated Parmesan
   cheese

Angel hair pasta

Need a romantic dinner for two? Or just something different? This buttermilk marinade will amaze you. It not only tenderizes the meat but tames wild duck flavor for the most discriminating of tastes. Personally, I like this recipe because the flattened breast cooks so quickly. Any recipe that makes me look good without having to break a sweat is a winner in my book.

### PREPARATION

1 Marinate the duck breasts in the buttermilk 12-36 hours.

### COOKING

1 Drain off marinade and discard buttermilk. Rinse and dry the breast meat. Flatten out with a meat mallet (carefully), between two pieces of plastic wrap to prevent tearing (to about $1/8$ inch thick). Rub with salt, pepper, and flour and set aside.

2 In a large skillet, melt the butter and olive oil over medium-high heat, stir garlic into the mixture, then add the flattened breasts and sauté until golden brown, about 3 minutes a side.

3 Remove the meat from the pan, and keep warm. Pour off any remaining butter and add the lemon juice, white wine, and capers to the pan. Lower heat to medium-low and stir gently until the sauce is reduced by about half, about 5-8 minutes. When the sauce is a deep golden brown, pour over the breasts and serve with Parmesan cheese over spaghetti or angel hair pasta. ❖

# CIPPOLINI ONION AND FRESH THYME STUFFED DUCK BREAST OVER CANNELLINI BEANS AND WILTED SWISS CHARD RAGOUT

SERVES 4

## INGREDIENTS

### FOR THE RAGOUT

1$\frac{1}{2}$ cups dry canellini beans

1 medium yellow onion, chopped

6 cloves garlic, sliced thin

1 leek, sliced thin

$\frac{1}{2}$ cup sliced celery

2 fresh bay leaves (or 1 dried)

$\frac{1}{8}$ cup olive oil

4 cups unsalted chicken or
    duck stock

3 roma tomatoes, diced small

Kosher salt

Black pepper

1 bunch Swiss chard, stems and
    spines removed, chopped

Eric Sharpe grew up hunting and fishing in Montana. He's also a graduate of the Culinary Institute of America. What this means is that there's a great cook out there who is creating exquisite gourmet dishes using honest-to-goodness, shot-at-and-hit game meat. The exact same game meat you and I have in our freezers. No need to adjust anything. Eric is totally wild in the kitchen.

### COOKING THE BEAN RAGOUT

1 Cover dry beans with water and soak overnight. The next day, drain the beans, and set aside.

2 In a medium-sized skillet over medium heat, sauté the onions, garlic, leek, celery, and bay leaf in the oil, 3 minutes, making sure they don't brown. Add the beans, stock, and tomatoes. Simmer over low heat until the beans are tender but not falling apart, about 45 minutes. Season to taste with salt and pepper.

### COOKING THE DUCK BREASTS

1 In a large skillet, sauté the onions in $\frac{1}{4}$ cup of the oil, tossing lightly, over medium heat, until the onions are soft and slightly caramelized, about 15-20 minutes. Add the sliced garlic and cook 1 minute more. Add $\frac{1}{2}$ tablespoon salt, a pinch of pepper and remove the onions from the heat. Let it sit at room temperature.

2 When the onion mixture is cool, combine with the ricotta and fresh thyme. Mix thoroughly.

3 Trim any excess fat or silver skin from the duck. Insert a small paring knife lengthways into the duck, making sure not to go all the way through. Spin the knife, carefully, making a pocket in the duck about 2-3 inches long.

ROTISSERIE DUCK
*recipe page 45*

TEXAS TWISTER SPLIT TEAL
*recipe page 70*

TRADITIONAL
STUFFED DUCKS
|*recipe page 39*

SWEET POTATO AND
PECAN STUFFED DUCKS
|*recipe page 41*

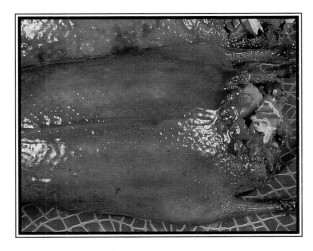

**WILD RICE, MALLARD,
AND MUSHROOM SOUP**
*|recipe page 26*

**BLUEBIRD SKY CHIRIZO**
*|recipe page 93*

SOUTH-OF-THE-BORDER
GOOSE STUFFING
[recipe page 51]

MINCED FRUIT DUCK
*recipe page 42*

**BEST-DRESSED GOOSE**
*|recipe page 55*

**EASY WAY TO MAKE
PEPPERONI STICKS**
*|recipe page 106*

DUCK & GOOSE COOKERY

**LET THEM EAT LEGS**
*|recipe page 86*

**TENDER MOLE LEGS**
*|recipe page 81*

CURRIED CROCK
|recipe page 82

THYME-STUFFED DUCK BREAST
*recipe page 68*

**GOOSE WITH
LINGONBERRY SAUCE**
*|recipe page 52*

**QUACKING GOOD
OVEN BREAKFAST**
*|recipe page 89*

**BLIND CHILI**
*|recipe page 33*

**SNOW GOOSE TENDER CHUNKS**
*|recipe page 12*

ITALIAN SAUSAGE WEDGIE
*recipe page 91*

WINGED PEPPERONI STICKS
*recipe page 106*

**LAYERED MEATLOAF**
*|recipe page 85*

**ITALIAN FENNEL SAUSAGE**
*|recipe page 90*

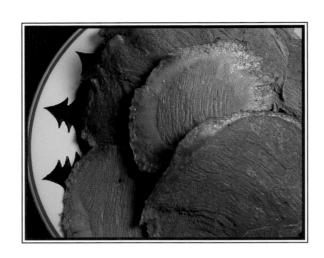

**WATER-SMOKED
GOOSE**
*\recipe page 116*

**INSIDE-OUT STUFFED GOOSE**
*\recipe page 63*

**4** Stuff the ricotta-onion mixture into the pocket, making sure there is enough to fill the cavity, without overflowing. Season the outside of the duck breast liberally with salt and pepper.

**5** In a large skillet, on medium-high heat, sear the breasts in the rest of the olive oil, until medium-rare, about 4 minutes each side. Remove from the pan and place on a warmed platter. Cover with a clean dry towel for 5 minutes.

### TO ASSEMBLE

Slice the duck breasts across the grain into medallions. Stir the Swiss chard into the ragout, and transfer to a warm platter. Lay the medallions on the ragout and serve.

### ABOUT LEEKS

For the most part it will help to imagine a large green onion: Cut off the roots. Then trim off the tough green tops of the leek, leaving about 6 inches of the freshest part of the leek—white and green—for cooking. Once trimmed, slice the leek lengthwise down the middle and rinse the sand carefully from the layers. (This is, after all, a root vegetable, and being more loosely stacked than a green onion allows some sand and dirt between the layers.) Dry well, then slice crossways for cooking. ❖

**TIP** Cannellini beans are a large Italian white bean (also known as a large kidney bean), which is also available already soaked and cooked, in a can. Though not as firm and good tasting as soaking them yourself, canned beans make the side dish go together very quickly.

# TEXAS TWISTER SPLIT TEAL

SERVES 2

### INGREDIENTS

2 teaspoons Texas Twister
   ground jalapeño seasoning

4 tablespoons honey

2 split teal (or one mallard,
   split)

Sometimes dinner needs to be easier than 1-2-3. Literally. When that happens, take advantage of the mountains of premixed spices available over the Web and in grocery stores. Here, I've mixed a bit of honey with Winchester's Texas Twister spice mix to add a bit of sweetness to the barbecue, but the easiest thing is to just rub the spices on the skin and go. The splitting part is easy, too. With a pair of poultry shears, clip the spine from the carcass, then open the rib cage, pressing apart the connection between the wishbone and sternum. Voila—a flat, almost-whole duck that's perfect for quick grilling.

COOKING

1 Combine the jalapeño seasoning and honey in a small bowl and mix thoroughly. Spread on the outside of the teal. (If you like, let it sit in the fridge overnight.)

2 Preheat your barbecue to medium-hot.

3 Set the teal skin-side up on the grill. Grill about 4 minutes a side for rare, 6 for medium, turning halfway through the cooking. (Be sure to pack a water pistol for putting out fat flare-ups. There's nothing worse than a charred teal.) Serve with grilled corn on the cob. ❖

TIP You can order Winchester's Texas Twister spice mix directly from the maker, Brooks Seasoning, Inc., at P.O. Box 140936, Irving, Texas 75014 (972-255-1115).

# CURRIED DUCK

**SERVES 4**

## INGREDIENTS

1 tablespoon cornstarch

1 tablespoon cold pineapple juice

1 tablespoon oil

1 tablespoon minced red onion

2 cloves garlic, minced

$1/2$ teaspoon Thai red curry paste

$1/2$ teaspoon curry powder

$3/4$ cup coconut milk

1 pound breast meat, in $3/4$-inch cubes

1 cup pineapple chunks, drained

$1/2$ cup half-and-half

This curry is one of those dishes that takes longer to explain than to cook—and it's designed for those of us who enjoy curry without actually having to eat fire. If you want to up the heat, double—or even triple—the red curry paste and curry powder. And feel free to use any mild-tasting dabbling duck or a goose for this dish.

## COOKING

1 In a small bowl, stir the cornstarch into the cold pineapple juice until all the lumps are dissolved. Set aside.

2 In a large skillet or wok, heat the oil over high heat. Add the onion and garlic and stir until lightly browned, about 2 minutes. Add the curry paste, curry powder, coconut milk and cook, stirring constantly until the mixture comes to a boil. Add the meat chunks, pineapple chunks, half-and-half, and cornstarch and juice mixture. When the mixture returns to a boil, reduce heat to low and simmer 15 minutes, until the sauce thickens and the meat is cooked through. ❖

# JAY'S DIPPING STRIPS

SERVES 2

## INGREDIENTS

Breasts of 2 mallard-sized ducks
   (or 1 pound meat)
750 ml bottle cheap champagne
$1/2$ cup vegetable oil
$1/2$ cup peanut oil
1 cup bread crumbs
$1/2$ teaspoon salt
$1/2$ teaspoon ground black pepper

My friend Jay is an avid elk hunter. But last fall he had very good luck in the duck blind. So it was no surprise when he invited his friends in for his specialty dish, which he made with delicious, grain-fed Alberta mallards instead of the usual elk. The only change? He added hot Chinese mustard to the array of dipping sauces.

MARINADE
Slice the meat into strips, about $1/4$ inch thick, 1-2 inches wide. Be sure to cut across the grain to make the meat as tender as possible. Toss the strips into a large bowl, and pour the champagne over them. Cover and let marinate for 1-2 hours at room temperature.

COOKING
   1 In a large skillet, heat the oil to medium to medium-high heat.
   2 While the oil heats, drain the marinade off and discard. Dry the strips of meat off on paper towels. In a plastic bag, combine the bread crumbs, salt, and pepper. Shake the meat in the bag, about $1/4$ pound at a time.
   3 Brown the strips, turning when you see blood start to seep through the tops of the strips, about 2-3 minutes a side. Then drain on paper towels.
   4 Serve hot, with prepared dipping sauces. Jay's favorites are sweet-and-sour, chili sauce, ranch dressing, a honey barbecue sauce, and hot Chinese mustard. ❖

# HOT PINEAPPLE KABOBS

**MAKES 4 FULL KABOBS**

### INGREDIENTS

1 pound dabbler breasts

$^1/_4$ teaspoon cumin

$^1/_2$ teaspoon garlic salt

$^1/_4$ teaspoon red pepper flakes

$^1/_4$ teaspoon ground black pepper

20-ounce can sliced pineapple (unsweetened)

1 tablespoon red wine vinegar

4 strips bacon

Here's a summer freezer-cleaning recipe that can serve as both appetizer and full-course meal. For dinner, serve with rice. Or, on really hot evenings, just roast some vegetables on the grill as well.

### PREPARATION

**1** Cut the duck into bite-sized pieces, across the grain. Pat dry with paper towels. Combine the cumin, garlic salt, red and black peppers and sprinkle onto duck. Press the spices into the meat with the back of a spoon, and let sit 5 minutes.

**2** Meanwhile, drain the juice off the canned pineapple. Save the slices. Combine the juice with the red wine vinegar. Then add the seasoned meat. Let marinate at least overnight—or up to a week in the refrigerator.

### COOKING

**1** Preheat the barbecue to medium-high heat. Thread the duck bites and sliced pineapple alternately onto skewers, then loosely wrap a slice of bacon around each kabob. Anchor it to the end of the skewer. Or place the duck and pineapple bits in hinged barbecue baskets, and drape the bacon across them. Discard the marinade.

**2** Grill the kabobs about 12 minutes, turning often, until the meat is medium-rare to medium. Serve with grilled vegetables. (Whole cherry or plum tomatoes, with chunks of green and red peppers, onion, and zucchini brushed lightly with olive oil, in a hinged grate, will cook about as fast as the kabobs.) ❖

# SWEET-AND-SOUR DUCK

**SERVES 4**

## INGREDIENTS

2 pounds duck meat,
  cut in small cubes
20$\frac{1}{2}$-ounce can of pineapple
  chunks (in pineapple juice,
  not syrup)
1 tablespoon soy sauce
1 clove garlic, minced
$\frac{1}{2}$ teaspoon salt
$\frac{1}{2}$ teaspoon ginger
1 tablespoon oil
$\frac{1}{2}$ cup sugar
2 tablespoons cornstarch
1 cup water
$\frac{1}{2}$ cup vinegar
1 green pepper, chopped
$\frac{1}{2}$ cup chopped green onions
4 cups cooked rice

*Good s/s sauce*

Sharon Gelhaus is married to an avid sportsman. And she raises and trains horses. So when it comes to cooking, she prefers recipes that not only take care of themselves—but the big old northern ducks Jim tends to bring home, too. This is Sharon and Jim's favorite way to tenderize a mature mallard. The best thing is, it also works for tender mallards and any goose. You just need about 2 pounds of meat.

## COOKING

**1** Dry the pieces of duck with paper towels. Drain the juice off the pineapple chunks, saving the juice and the pineapple chunks. In a large bowl, combine $\frac{1}{2}$ cup of the juice, soy sauce, garlic, salt, and ginger. Mix well and set aside.

**2** In a large skillet, heat the oil over medium heat and lightly brown the cubed duck. Once browned, pour the pineapple juice and soy sauce mixture over the duck. Bring the pan to a boil, lower heat to simmer, and cover. Simmer for 1 hour 15 minutes, stirring now and then, or until all the liquid is absorbed.

**3** Remove the duck from the pan. Pour off excess fat. Combine the sugar, cornstarch, remaining pineapple juice, water, and vinegar and add to pan drippings. Cook until quite shiny and thickened over medium heat, stirring constantly, 4-6 minutes.

**4** When thickened, add the pineapple chunks, green pepper, and green onions to the sauce. Heat through, and add the duck chunks. Serve on a bed of rice. ❖

*35 minutes too low tough meat*

# SZECHUAN STIR-FRY

SERVES 2-4

## INGREDIENTS

1 fat mallard, skinned and boned

1 tablespoon soy sauce

1 tablespoon sake

2 teaspoons hoisin sauce

2 tablespoons oil

3 cloves garlic, minced

Zest of 1 tangerine

1 cup broccoli florets, separated

2 medium carrots,
   sliced very thin

2 green onions, chopped

## FOR THE SAUCE

Juice of 1 tangerine

1 tablespoon soy sauce

1 tablespoon sake

$1/2$ teaspoon Chinese chili sauce

$1/4$ teaspoon crushed Szechuan
   peppers

2 tablespoons cornstarch

This recipe calls for a nice, fat mallard, but because of the combination of very strong spices and the marinade, you can also use a smaller diving duck that you may be afraid to use in some other, less spicy recipes. Whichever you use, make sure you have $1^1/_2$-2 pounds of duck meat so you'll satisfy 2-4 hungry people. (If you can't get hold of any sake (Japanese rice wine) a medium-dry sherry will work. The better the quality, the better the finish...but you are cooking with pretty heavy-duty spices here. Just don't fall for the "cooking" sherry.)

### PREPARATION

1 Cut the duck up into strips—$^1/_4$ inch thick, 1-2 inches long, and $^1/_2$ inch wide.

2 In a large bowl, combine the soy sauce, sake, hoisin sauce, and 2 teaspoons of the oil. Stir the duck strips into this marinade, cover tightly, and refrigerate overnight.

### COOKING

1 Combine the sauce ingredients in a small bowl, including the cornstarch. Stir well to combine, and set aside. Pour off the marinade and save. Dry the duck pieces with paper towels.

2 Heat 1 tablespoon of the oil in a wok (or large, heavy-bottomed skillet) until it just begins to smoke. Add the duck strips and cook until just browning, about 2 minutes. Transfer duck strips to a warm platter. Add the rest of the oil to the wok and sauté the garlic and tangerine peel for 10-15 seconds, then add the broccoli and carrots. Cook these 4-5 minutes until softened, and add the green onions.

3 Return duck strips to wok, and pour in sauce. Stir to coat the vegetables and duck strips and cook until the sauce thickens. Serve over rice. ❖

# MILLENNIUM STIR-FRY

SERVES 4-6

## INGREDIENTS

1 cup beef bouillon

$1/4$ cup soy sauce

$1/4$ cup honey

$1/4$ cup rice wine vinegar

1 teaspoon grated fresh ginger

$1^1/2$ pounds sliced breast meat

$1/4$ cup oil

1 medium onion, thinly sliced

1 stalk celery, thinly sliced

$1/2$ red sweet pepper, sliced

1 cup pea pods

4 cups cooked rice

At our house, stir-fries are a favorite winter meal. But over the years the sauce has changed. The previous recipe is more like my old standby, with a thickened sauce. But this next one is my new favorite. Try it this way once, but if you miss the traditional, thicker sauce, just dissolve 1 teaspoon of cornstarch into 2 tablespoons of cold water when you chop up the vegetables. Then add the slurry into the sauce the last minute or two of cooking. It will thicken up nicely.

### PREPARATION

Combine in a medium bowl: bouillon, soy sauce, honey, wine vinegar, and ginger. Add sliced meat, and stir gently. Cover the bowl and refrigerate 1-4 hours.

### COOKING

1 Pour off the marinade into another bowl and save it. Dry the meat slices with paper towels. Heat the oil to just below the smoking point, over medium-high to high heat, and quickly stir-fry the slices of meat. Remove the meat, and stir-fry the onion, celery, and red sweet pepper until it begins to soften, about 5 minutes.

2 Add the meat back into the pan, add the marinade, and reduce the heat to low. Let the mixture simmer about 8 minutes until the sauce is reduced by about half. Add pea pods and toss until just warm. Serve over rice. ❖

# GOOSE BREAST WITH SAUERKRAUT

SERVES 6-8

## INGREDIENTS

Breasts of 2 Canada geese,
    skinned
2 tablespoons bacon fat
4 cups sauerkraut
$1/2$ cup dry white wine
$1/2$ cup minced onion
$1/2$ teaspoon salt
$1/2$ teaspoon pepper
1 teaspoon dried leaf thyme
1 teaspoon whole caraway seeds
$1/2$ cup heavy cream

Here's a perfect recipe for those who skin and breast-out geese—and cook all the pink out of birds. (It's also good cooked with the pink still there.) The bacon adds lots of moisture to the meat; the sauerkraut neutralizes wild flavors. (See the leg recipes at the end of this recipe section for delicious ways to cook the rest of the bird.)

COOKING

1 Preheat the oven to 325 F. In a 5-quart Dutch oven, (or a heavy-bottomed, tightly covered baking dish) brown the breasts in the bacon fat over medium-high heat. When all sides are browned, remove the goose and add the sauerkraut, white wine, onion, salt, pepper, thyme, and caraway seeds to the pot. Stir up the pan juices into the new additions, so everything is well coated.

2 Return the breasts to the pot, nestling them into the sauerkraut mixture. Cover the Dutch oven and place in the center of the pre-heated oven. Bake about 90 minutes, until tender.

3 To serve, remove the goose breasts from the Dutch oven and stir the cream into the sauerkraut. Slice the breasts and place them on a heated platter. Arrange the sauerkraut around them. Serve with boiled potatoes tossed in butter and minced parsley. For a real treat, slice up 2 or 3 apples and sauté them in a little butter with sugar and cinnamon to taste. The apples make a great side dish for these sauerkraut breasts. ❖

# WATERFOWL CARNITA

**SERVES 4**

### INGREDIENTS

**FOR THE MARINADE**

1 orange, quartered

1 cup Coca-Cola

2 cloves minced garlic

1 teaspoon ground cumin

1 teaspoon dried minced onion

1 teaspoon black pepper

$\frac{1}{2}$ teaspoon salt

$\frac{1}{2}$ teaspoon dried leaf oregano

$\frac{1}{2}$ teaspoon chili powder

1 pound duck or goose breast

**FOR COOKING AND SERVING**

4 tablespoons oil

4 flour tortillas

1 cup salsa

1 cup refried beans

2 cups shredded lettuce

Remember seventh grade, when you put a chicken bone in a glass of soda? And it lost all its starch? Well, the Coke in this recipe tenderizes breast meat in the same way. So use an old goose or mallard. And expect great flavor as well.

### PREPARATION

In a deep bowl, squeeze the juice from the orange quarters into the Coca-Cola and add the peels, garlic, cumin, onion, pepper, salt, oregano, and chili powder. Stir to mix, then submerge the breast meat into the marinade. Cover and refrigerate overnight.

### COOKING

1 Two hours before serving: Pour the marinade off and save it. Dry the meat with paper towels.

2 In a large skillet, heat the oil to medium-high heat. Add the whole breasts and sear the outside of the meat until well browned. Add the marinade, turn the heat down to low, cover the pot, and simmer until tender. Or transfer everything to a Crock-Pot and cook on low 7-8 hours. Add more Coke if needed to keep the meat covered as it cooks.

To serve, remove the meat from the skillet and shred it with a fork. Wrap in flour tortillas with salsa, refried beans, and shredded lettuce. ❖

# DELICIOUSLY DIFFERENT CROCK-O-LEGS

SERVES 4-6

## INGREDIENTS

### FOR THE SAUCE
1½ cups pitted prunes
1½ cups water
1 cup sliced onion
2 cloves garlic
1 teaspoon salt
¼ teaspoon pepper
½ teaspoon ground ginger
5 tablespoons cider vinegar
1 tablespoon honey

### FOR THE LEGS
1 12-ounce lager beer
2 pounds legs

I have used this sauce to slow-cook everything from buffalo ribs to snow goose legs. It's a spicy sauce with lots of tang, and the long, moist cooking method is perfect for tenderizing the toughest of cuts. Use any waterfowl legs you want, or substitute a goose breast or two. Here we'll use it on a pile of legs. (If you want, prepare the sauce up to a week in advance and store in a covered container in the refrigerator.)

### PREPARATION
1 In a 2-quart saucepan, combine the prunes, water, onion, garlic, salt, pepper, and ginger. Bring to a boil, then turn down to low heat and simmer uncovered for 15 minutes. Let cool just enough to transfer to a food processor.

2 In the processor, add the vinegar and honey to the spiced prune mixture and purée until smooth. You can refrigerate the sauce, covered, up to a week. It should make about 2½ cups of sauce.

### TO COOK THE LEGS
1 In a Crock-Pot, stir the sauce and beer together and fold the legs into the mixture. Cover and cook on low for 8 hours.

2 In the oven, combine the sauce and beer in a 9x13 inch baking pan and nestle the legs into the sauce. Add more beer if needed, to immerse the legs. Cover tightly with foil or lid and bake at 300 F for 90 minutes, or until tender. Serve with egg noodles. ❖

# SAUCY LEGS

SERVES 3-4

### INGREDIENTS

1 16-ounce bottle Russian
   dressing
1 cup apricot jam
1 package onion soup mix
1 pound duck legs

I first heard about this recipe down at my post office from another woman who hunts ducks. Then, before I could try it, I heard variations on the theme from Utah and Michigan. It's an easy way to soften up a variety of waterfowl legs, mallard-sized and larger, and works as a main dish or an appetizer.

COOKING

1 Preheat oven to 350 F. Combine the Russian dressing, jam, and soup mix in a baking dish or Dutch oven. Toss the legs in the sauce mixture.

2 Cover and bake 90 minutes. Serve hot with red cabbage. ❖

TIP To use as an appetizer, separate the thigh from the lower leg. Then slice through the lower leg tendons at the "ankle." The lower leg meat will form a tasty "lollipop" at the top of the shin bone.

# TENDER MOLE LEGS

**SERVES 6-8**

## INGREDIENTS

6 tablespoons oil, divided

2 medium onions, chopped

6 cloves garlic, minced

2 teaspoons dried leaf marjoram

2 tablespoons dried leaf cilantro

1 teaspoon sugar

1 pound assorted duck legs

2 14-ounce cans red enchilada
    sauce

2 14.5-ounce cans diced
    tomatoes

2 sweet potatoes, diced

2 tablespoons prepared mole
    sauce

1 teaspoon cinnamon

2 teaspoons salt

I ran into mole sauce the last time I visited Brownsville, Texas. Real mole (pronounced moh-lay) sauce is a days-long process to make, but this bottled version is a good substitute at the end of a hard day afield.

COOKING

1 In a large skillet, heat 2 tablespoons of the oil over medium heat and lightly sauté the onion and garlic. Once golden, stir in the marjoram and cilantro. Heat until you smell the spices, about 2-3 minutes. Transfer the mixture to the Crock-Pot. Add the rest of the oil to the skillet, and the sugar. Lightly brown both sides of the legs, about 3-4 minutes a side. Put them in the Crock-Pot, too.

2 Add the enchilada sauce, tomatoes, diced sweet potatoes, mole, cinnamon, and salt. Stir the mixture in the Crock-Pot until mixed. Cover the crock, set on low, and let cook 6-8 hours. Serve on rice with sour cream and avocado slices. ❖

# CURRIED CROCK

**SERVES 4-6**

### INGREDIENTS

16 ounces lager beer

1 $\frac{1}{3}$ cup apricot juice

$\frac{3}{4}$ cup cream

3 tablespoons brown sugar

3 teaspoons lime juice

2 teaspoons sweet paprika

1 teaspoon curry powder

1 teaspoon dried onion flakes

1 teaspoon salt

$\frac{1}{2}$ teaspoon black pepper

1$\frac{1}{2}$-2 pounds skinned
   duck legs or breasts (or thighs
   and drumsticks of geese)

1 teaspoon oil

A recipe for any part of any bird will always become a favorite at our house. Start the whole thing at once and cook it overnight, or while you're at work. The best part is that the breast of a wild bird can cook as long as the legs without getting "gummy," as commercially raised chicken breasts will get. Feel free to double or triple the recipe, but don't skimp on the sauce—you'll want lots.

COOKING

1 In a 3-quart Crock-Pot, combine the beer, juice, cream, brown sugar, lime juice, paprika, curry powder, onion flakes, salt, and pepper. Stir to mix well. Turn Crock-Pot on to low heat

2 In a skillet over medium heat, sauté the legs and breasts in oil until just starting to brown, 2-3 minutes. Drain on paper towels a few seconds, then transfer to Crock-Pot. When all the meat is browned, stir the pot so that everything is well coated with the curry sauce. Cover the crock and cook 6-8 hours, until the meat is tender.

3 Serve over rice, or with white or sweet potatoes that have been cooked, diced, and then tossed in the curry sauce. ❖

# DUCK ITALIANO

SERVES 2

## INGREDIENTS

1 pound filleted breast
   (about 1 fat mallard)
1 tablespoon bacon grease
1 large yellow onion, sliced thin
4 cloves garlic, minced
28-ounce can diced,
   peeled tomatoes
6-8 shakes red pepper Tabasco
   sauce
$1/2$ teaspoon salt
$1/2$ teaspoon black pepper
4 cups cooked pasta
2 ounces prosciutto (or ham),
   sliced into thin strips
$1/4$ cup grated Parmesan cheese

I ran into this recipe at a Ducks Unlimited banquet last fall. It's from the wife of our local vet, who is a full-time nurse as well as a great cook. The way Jackie told it, she made the recipe in a pressure cooker, on low for 60 minutes. Since my pressure cooker's gasket is too old to use, and too obscure to replace, I made it in a Dutch oven, cooking it in the oven at moderate temperature. Feel free to do it either way. And feel free to substitute legs for breasts. This is one of those recipes that cooks long and wet and eventually makes every-thing tender.

### COOKING

1 Preheat oven to 300 F. In a 5-quart Dutch oven or heavy-bottomed (covered) casserole brown the duck breast in the bacon grease, over medium heat, then add the onions and garlic to the pot and sauté until tender, about 4 minutes. Add the tomatoes, Tabasco, salt, and pepper, stirring to combine the sauce completely, and let it come back to a low boil.

2 Bury the thighs and drumsticks in the sauce, cover the pot, and place in the center of your oven. Cook for 60 minutes, or until the meat is tender.

3 Serve over a bed of pasta, or spaghetti squash with strips of prosciutto (or ham) and grated Parmesan cheese.

### TO COOK SPAGHETTI SQUASH

If you're tired of pasta, or are on one of those high-protein/low-carb diets, spaghetti squash is a nice change of pace. More nutritious than pasta, it has a slightly sweet, nutty flavor that goes nicely with waterfowl. It's as easy to grow in your garden as zucchini, but unlike zucchini it's a winter squash. Cut it off the vine and store it in the basement and it will keep for several months. Spaghetti squash also cooks up quickly in the microwave. Allow about $^3/_4$-1 cup for each serving.

**1** Cut a medium-sized spaghetti squash into 1-inch slices (about 5 inches in diameter). Clean the seeds and loose hair (as you would prepare a Jack-O-Lantern or cantaloupe) and place the slices on a plate. Cover loosely with plastic wrap and microwave on high (700 watts) for about 5 minutes, or until the meat pulls away from the rind easily with a fork. Remove the plastic wrap and let cool a few minutes, so it's easier to handle.

**2** Remove the meat from the rind, gently, with a fork. If it doesn't "string" like spaghetti, cook it 1-2 minutes more. It's now ready to eat. Each 1-inch slice (5 inches diameter squash) will provide about $^3/_4$ cup of cooked spaghetti squash, enough for 1 serving. ❖

# LAYERED MEATLOAF

SERVES 4-6

## INGREDIENTS

8 ounces ground goose meat

8 ounces ground chicken

1 egg, lightly beaten

1 teaspoon chicken bouillon
   granules

1/2 cup water

2 teaspoons Worcestershire
   Sauce

1 cup dried bread crumbs

1/2 teaspoon dried leaf thyme

1/2 teaspoon dried leaf basil

1/2 teaspoon dried leaf oregano

1 teaspoon salt

1/2 teaspoon black pepper

1/8 teaspoon cayenne pepper

1/2 cup chopped onion

10 3/4-ounce can tomato purée

2 tomatoes, sliced

8 ounces mozzarella cheese,
   sliced

My friend Bill Buckley, wildlife photographer and frequent contributor to *Ducks Unlimited* magazine, suggested this recipe to me. But when he makes it, he presses out the ground meat mixture on waxed paper, arranges the tomatoes and cheese slices on top, and rolls the meat loaf—much like a jelly roll. Do it that way or layer it, as I've done here.

### COOKING

1 Preheat oven to 400 F. In a large bowl, combine the two meats with the egg. In another smaller bowl, dissolve the chicken granules in the water, add the Worcestershire Sauce, add this mixture to the meats, and stir to combine. Add the bread crumbs, thyme, basil, oregano, salt, black pepper, cayenne pepper, and mix thoroughly. Add the chopped onions and mix them well.

2 To assemble the meat loaf: Spread about 1/3 of the tomato purée in the bottom of a 9x5 inch loaf pan. Arrange one layer of tomato slices in the purée. Spread one half of the meat loaf mixture over the tomatoes, then arrange another single layer of tomatoes and a layer of one half of the mozzarella cheese slices over the meat mixture. Spread the second half of the meat in the pan, then top with tomato slices, cheese slices, and the rest of the purée.

3 Bake for 50 minutes, then let stand about 5 minutes to settle. Serve with home-fried potatoes tossed with Kosher salt. ❖

# LET THEM EAT LEGS

SERVES 4

## INGREDIENTS

### FOR THE MARINADE

2 teaspoons chicken soup base

2 cups water

2 tablespoons soy sauce

1 tablespoon medium-dry sherry

2 tablespoons creamy peanut
   butter

1/4 teaspoon garlic powder

1 teaspoon crushed red pepper
   flakes (or less, to taste)

8 ounces boned leg meat

### FOR THE COOKING

2/3 cup sliced celery

2/3 cup sliced carrot

2/3 cup cooked rice

2 teaspoons chicken soup base

2 cups hot water

The easiest way I know of to cut leg meat from the bone is by poultry shears. Start with a skinned leg. Then clip the tendons that attach each muscle group to the joints. Slide the point of the poultry shears between the bone and the meat, and clip the meat free of the bone. Finally, trim away all fat, sinew, and bloodshot meat. Two to 3 average-sized snow geese (or 4-6 mallards or 1-2 Canadas) will provide enough meat for this soup.

### TO MAKE THE MARINADE

1 In a medium saucepan, combine the soup base, water, soy sauce, sherry, peanut butter, garlic powder, and pepper flakes. Bring to a boil and simmer until the sauce is completely mixed, about 10 minutes. Let cool.

2 Cut the leg meat into bite-sized pieces and place in a resealable plastic bag. When the peanut butter mixture has cooled to room temperature, add it to the meat. Seal the bag and shake well to coat all the pieces. Marinate in the refrigerator overnight.

### TO COOK THE SOUP

1 Pour the marinade off into a 5-quart soup pot. Bring the marinade to a boil and drop the meat into the boiling marinade, a few pieces at a time, so the pot keeps boiling. (No need to dry the meat.) Cover the pot, reduce heat to a simmer, and cook the meat 20 minutes.

2 Add the celery, carrot, rice, and additional soup base and water to the meat mixture and bring the pot back to a boil. Immediately lower the heat to simmer, and cover the pot. Simmer about another 10 minutes and serve. ❖

TIP Pepper lovers, beware! You may be used to adding more pepper before you even start cooking, especially if you've cooked from my cookbooks before. But this recipe even made my husband, John, sit back. For those who want to try the recipe but are a little cautious, halve the red pepper flakes the first time you cook this up. That's where the heat comes from in this recipe. If you find you want more heat, you can always add more pepper flakes.

TIP The chicken soup "base" used in this recipe is a less salty, more chicken-flavored substitute for the chicken bouillon we are more used to. It also dissolves a lot more easily than bouillon cubes and granules. And with all the other salt in this recipe (soy sauce, peanut butter) the soup base is a better choice. You can find soup base in a lot of grocery stores, in the soup aisle, but it can also be ordered from The Spice House, a mail-order spice catalog (414-272-0977) or direct from McCormick (800-322-SPICE).

DUCK

&

GOOSE

# SAUSAGES
# & JERKY

COOKERY

# QUACKING GOOD BREAKFAST SAUSAGE

MAKES ³/₄ POUND

## INGREDIENTS

¼ **pound duck or goose meat**

¼ **pound boneless,**
   **skinless chicken breast**

¼ **pound pork**

³/₄ **teaspoon salt**

½ **teaspoon pepper**

¼ **teaspoon ground sage**

¼ **teaspoon ground thyme**

To make sausage, I use what I have the most of. Some years it's mallards, some years geese. I use chicken breast to stretch my recipe, and pork to add a bit of sweet fat to the pot. And of course, once you add pork, you need to cook the sausage until all the pink has disappeared, whether for the table or when testing the flavor.

PREPARATION

Grind the meats together through the coarse plate of your grinder. Combine with the salt, pepper, sage, thyme and grind once more. Cover and chill 2-3 hours to allow the flavors to develop.

COOKING

Shape into patties and fry in a hot pan or check out the recipe that follows for an easy, stick-to-your-ribs meal. ❖

### HOG OR LAMB? HOW SHOULD I CASE MY SAUSAGE?

The size of casings is up to you. That's one of the joys of making them yourself. But there are certain traditions among sausage people. For instance, I have no problem with dogs in hog casings, even though most commercial dogs are in smaller-diameter tubes. But breakfast sausage is another thing. That "should" always be either patties or lamb-sized casings, but lamb-sized casings are not always as easy to find as hog casings. It's personal. Do what you want. Do what's easy. And if you really want to make a science of it, look up on the Internet for sausage-making supplies. It all depends on how much time you want to spend preparing the things. Personally, I'm more interested in the eating.

How much casing you need is easy. Allow about 1 foot of hog casing per pound of meat ground, then add another foot for insurance. It's always better to have too much hog casing than too little when you're all set up to stuff your sausage. For lamb casings, allow about 50 percent more length per pound. ∎

# QUACKING GOOD OVEN BREAKFAST

SERVES 4

## INGREDIENTS

4 tablespoons oil

$^3/_4$ pound breakfast sausage
(from previous recipe)

1 cup sliced onion

6 medium potatoes,
sliced $^1/_4$ inch thick

1 teaspoon salt

$^1/_2$ teaspoon white pepper

6 eggs

1 cup grated Cheddar cheese

I love one-dish meals that cook in the oven all on their own. This one makes a perfect brunch after you've been out in a chilly goose blind all morning—and takes only a few minutes to get started.

COOKING

1 Preheat the oven to 350 F. Heat the oil in a 5-quart Dutch oven, over medium-high heat. Brown the sausage, then add the onion, potatoes, salt, and pepper and toss. Cover the pot and transfer to the oven. Cook covered about 25-30 minutes, or until the potatoes are fork-tender.

2 To finish the dish, remove the lid. Break the eggs across the potatoes and cover the Dutch oven again. Cook another 7-10 minutes, until the eggs are done. Grate the cheese over the top and serve immediately. ❖

## TESTING SAUSAGE SAFELY

All of the sausage recipes in these pages contain pork or commercial chicken mixed with the wild waterfowl meat. The presence of these commercial ingredients means you should never taste the sausage raw—or even pink. But you do need to adjust the spices to your own tastes, both while mixing and after the flavors have "grown" in the refrigerator for 24 hours.

The easiest answer is to place about 1 teaspoon of the raw mix into a microwaveable cup. Cook on high (700 watts) for 1 minute, until the sizzling stops. Then slice the sausage in half to make sure there is no pink inside, and test for flavor.

The downside is that cooking in the microwave will make the sausage tough; but the upside is you won't risk illness from eating raw pork or chicken. Plus, the deep shape of the cup will keep your microwave clean. ■

# ITALIAN FENNEL SAUSAGE

MAKES 1¹/₂ POUNDS

### INGREDIENTS

¹/₂ pound duck or goose meat

¹/₂ pound boneless, skinless
   chicken breast

¹/₂ pound pork

2 teaspoons salt

1¹/₂ teaspoons black pepper

¹/₂ teaspoon red pepper flakes

2 teaspoons minced onion flakes

1¹/₂ teaspoons whole fennel seed

Ever go to the grocery store and buy "Italian" sausage that tasted more like brats? It's almost as frustrating as buying strawberries that have no more flavor than a potato. But you can do something about the sausage. Make your own. And then make the wedgie recipe that follows.

### PREPARATION

1 Trim all skin and fat off the waterfowl, then run all three meats through the coarse plate of your grinder. In a large bowl, mix the meats with the salt, black pepper, red pepper, onion flakes, and fennel seed. Run through the coarse plate one more time, then cover and refrigerate overnight.

2 Once the flavors have developed overnight, test a small amount of the sausage, by cooking in the microwave. Adjust flavor if necessary.

### COOKING

Preheat your barbecue to medium-high heat. Shape the sausage into patties and grill about 10 minutes to a side, putting out fat fires with a water pistol to prevent burning. Serve with pasta and a salad. Or make into a delicious sandwich, as in the recipe that follows. ❖

TIP When adding pork to a larger batch of sausage, the most economical cut, as well as the best in terms of meat vs. fat, is a picnic roast. The reason it's economical is that it's taken from the shoulder, a less tender cut of meat than loin, or even chops. However, if you are making a small batch of sausage, and you don't need 3-4 pounds of pork, just grind up 1 or 2 pork chops and throw them in. That will give you a good fat to meat ratio for a moderately paced 25-30 percent fat sausage mix.

# ITALIAN SAUSAGE WEDGIES

**SERVES 4**

## INGREDIENTS

1¹/₂ pounds Italian sausage

2 tablespoons butter

¹/₂ teaspoon dried leaf oregano

¹/₄ teaspoon garlic powder

4 large slices Italian bread

8-ounce bottle marinara sauce

1 cup grated Mozzarella cheese

¹/₄ cup grated Parmesan cheese

Meatball sandwiches have long been one of my favorite eat-out dishes. But then I figured out an easy way to bake the meatballs, and now it's a favorite at-home dish, perfect for parties or snacks. You can make the meatballs and serve them separately on a toothpick, or go to the extreme and make the perfect wedgie, hero, poor boy sandwich. Whatever you call it, it's delicious.

## COOKING

**1** Preheat the oven to 350 F. Shape the sausage into balls, about 1 tablespoon each, and place on a lightly oiled baking pan. Bake uncovered for 25 minutes, or until no longer pink inside.

**2** When the meatballs are done, remove from the oven and turn the oven to broil. Combine the butter with the oregano and garlic powder, and spread on one side of the bread. Broil, butter side up, 3-4 inches below the flame, until golden brown (about 5 minutes).

**3** To assemble: Spoon some marinara sauce over the toasted bread, then place the meatballs on top. Sprinkle with the mozzarella and Parmesan cheese, then slide back under the broiler until the cheese melts. Serve immediately. ❖

# PARMESAN ITALIAN SAUSAGE

**MAKES 1 POUND**

### INGREDIENTS

1 foot hog casings (1½-inch
 diameter)
8 ounces coarsely ground
 mallard
8 ounces coarsely ground
 chicken breast
½ cup chopped onion
¼ cup chopped green pepper
1 teaspoon salt
1 teaspoon white pepper
¼ cup grated Parmesan cheese

This is a more delicate Italian sausage that has incredible flavor with very little fat. Make it into a wedgie sandwich, as in the last recipe, or cook it whole in hog casings and serve with spaghetti and tomato sauce.

### COOKING

1 Prepare the casings according to package directions.

2 Mix the mallard and chicken meats well. Add the onion, green pepper, salt, white pepper, and Parmesan cheese. Mix well with your hands.

3 Stuff the mixture into casings, twisting off into 4-inch links. Or shape into patties.

4 To serve with spaghetti, place the cased sausages in a large skillet with water halfway up the sausages. Bring to a boil, then lower the heat to a simmer and cover the pot. When the water is almost all evaporated (about 30 minutes) brown the sausages on all sides and serve. ❖

# BLUEBIRD SKY CHORIZO

**MAKES 1 POUND**

## INGREDIENTS

¹/₂ **pound coarsely ground
waterfowl meat**

¹/₂ **pound coarsely ground
picnic roast**

1 **teaspoon garlic salt**

¹/₂ **teaspoon black pepper**

2 **teaspoons dried onion flakes**

2 **teaspoons chili powder**

4 **teaspoons minced fresh
cilantro leaves**

Chorizo is a fresh Mexican sausage that varies from region to region—and often, house to house. This one is my favorite, with fresh cilantro brightening the sausage. But don't underestimate the cilantro. It looks almost like parsley, but just brush the leaves as you stand in the produce section and it will immediately give off a bright, fresh aroma. Then tear a leaf in two; if it's fresh, you should feel the bite. Cook this chorizo as below, or slowly on the barbecue grill with 1 cup of mesquite wood chips thrown on the coals. Use the worst birds you have, because these spices will hide almost anything.

### COOKING

1 Mix the two meats well. Add the salt, black pepper, onion flakes, chili powder, and cilantro. Mix well with your hands.

2 Stuff the mixture into casings, or prepare as patties.

3 To cook: Fry over medium heat in just a little oil until all the pink is gone, about 10 minutes a side. Serve with refried beans and Spanish rice, or make into appetizers as in the next recipe. ❖

# CHORIZO IN A BLANKET

MAKES 16 PIGS

### INGREDIENTS

1 pound cased sausage
   (lamb-sized casings)
2 tubes refrigerator crescent
   rolls
1 egg, beaten

You can follow this appetizer variation with the Italian, Polish, or kielbasa sausage. Just pick the sausage to match your mood. The refrigerator rolls make this an easy-to-fix appetizer.

COOKING

1 Preheat oven to 375 F. In a large covered skillet, parboil the sausages over medium heat in water, about half-deep on the sausages. When the water is almost all evaporated, about 30 minutes, continue to cook on medium heat until the sausages are browned on all sides. Remove from skillet and set aside.

2 Unroll the crescent dough. Cut sausage into 16 pieces, equal to the number of crescent rolls you have. Place each sausage length on the narrow end of the crescent dough and roll up. Place tag end down and put on a cookie sheet. Brush each pig with the egg.

3 Bake in preheated oven, about 20 minutes or until the dough is golden brown. ❖

# BIG BLOW CHORIZO

MAKES 1 POUND

## INGREDIENTS

1/2 **pound ground waterfowl meat**

1/2 **pound ground picnic roast**

1 **tablespoon white vinegar**

2 **cloves garlic, minced**

1 **teaspoon paprika**

1 **teaspoon salt**

1/4 **teaspoon ground, dry habañero pepper**

As its name implies, Bluebird Sky Chorizo is a gentler recipe than this Big Blow Chorizo. Plus Big Blow Chorizo is designed with room to grow. The recipe below is how I like it. But if you like to eat spicy hot stuff, let 'er rip. Start by not re-hydrating the habañero pepper: Throw the whole dry pepper into a grinder, then it is easy to measure the heat. Use as little or as much as you want, testing the recipe as you go. Then, when you think it's right, let it sit in the refrigerator for 24 hours and test one more time. Too hot? Add more meat. Too mild? You're on your own.

### PREPARATION

1 In a large bowl, combine all the ingredients by hand, using rubber gloves. Shape into a ball and cover tightly with plastic wrap, pressing the wrap into the surface of the sausage.

2 Place the sausage in the refrigerator overnight, then retest for flavor. Place a 1-teaspoon ball of sausage in a cup and microwave on high (700 watts) for about 1 minute. To add heat, add habañero pepper; to tame the heat, add more of everything else.

3 When you are sure you have the right heat, you can stuff the chorizo into casings, or simply prepare them as patties. To store, double wrap in plastic wrap, then freezer paper. You can freeze sausage safely for up to 3 months.

### COOKING

1 Pan fry patties in a medium-hot skillet, with just a little oil until all the pink is gone (about 10-15 minutes). Cased sausage can be grilled over medium heat, about 10 minutes to a side, until the pink is all gone. Or slice the cased sausage and brown in a skillet and add it to your favorite chili recipe. ❖

# DUCK DOGS

MAKES 1 POUND

## INGREDIENTS

¹/₂ **pound ground waterfowl meat**

¹/₂ **pound picnic roast**

¹/₂ **cup chopped onion**

2 **cloves minced garlic**

1 **teaspoon celery salt**

¹/₄ **teaspoon cayenne pepper**

2 **tablespoons milk**

These are for the 2-legged hunter, not the 4-legged sidekick. One of the pleasures of making sausages at home is that you control the ingredients, and these Duck Dogs are an example. No lips, cheeks, snouts, or other by-products. This is all good meat, made into delicious hot dogs, and you can stuff the casings to any length—hang the dog a foot out of the roll if you want. These cooking directions are for hog casings 1¹/₂ inches in diameter. Lamb-sized casings (up to 1 inch) will take a little less time to cook.

## PREPARATION

1 Trim all skin and fat off the waterfowl, then run both meats through the coarse plate of your grinder. In a large bowl, mix the meats thoroughly with the onion, garlic, celery salt, cayenne pepper, and milk. Once mixed, run the mixture through the coarse plate of the grinder.

2 Stuff into casings. Prepare for the freezer by wrapping tightly in plastic wrap, then in freezer paper. Or vacuum seal. Freeze up to 3 months.

## COOKING

Grill over medium heat, or place in a pot of boiling water (see boiling sidebar on page 99). When the water comes back to a boil, reduce the heat to a slow simmer. Simmer about 20-25 minutes, until all the pink is gone. ❧

# GOOSE BRATWURSTS

**MAKES 2 POUNDS**

### INGREDIENTS

1 pound ground waterfowl meat

1 pound ground picnic roast

1 teaspoon ground allspice

1 teaspoon whole caraway seed

1 teaspoon dried leaf marjoram

1 teaspoon salt

1 teaspoon ground black pepper

1 12-ounce can of beer

This is my favorite way to eat brats, and one of the easiest. Get some good hard rolls and a variety of mustards and sauerkraut for a real treat.

### PREPARATION

1 In a large bowl, combine all the ingredients and mix well with your hands. Grind the whole recipe together, to mix the flavors well, on the coarse plate of your grinder.

2 Stuff into casings. Prepare for the freezer by wrapping tightly in plastic wrap, then in freezer paper. Or vacuum seal. Freeze for up to 3 months.

### COOKING

Place the cased sausage in a large skillet with the beer and enough water to make the liquid rise halfway up the sausage, over medium-high heat. When the water comes to a boil, turn the heat down to simmer and cover the skillet. Continue simmering until the liquid has evaporated (about 30 minutes), then brown the brats until dark brown. Serve with Gourmet Mac and Muenster à la Microwave, which follows. ❖

# GOURMET MAC AND MUENSTER À LA MICROWAVE

SERVES 4

## INGREDIENTS

1 cup milk

3 tablespoons all-purpose flour

3 tablespoons butter or
    margarine

1 cup grated Muenster cheese

1/4 cup grated Parmesan cheese

3 cups cooked pasta

This is my all-time favorite comfort dish. And the great thing about it is that it is so variable. Muenster and Parmesan cheese is the way I make it most frequently, but sometimes I add provolone or mild Cheddar instead. Feel free to substitute your favorite cheese, or make it as written. Either way, you'll be pleased to see what you can make by just boiling water and programming a microwave.

COOKING

1 In a large glass bowl, whisk the milk and flour until smooth. Add the butter, and microwave the mixture on high (700 watts) for about 2 minutes, until the sauce is thick, stopping and stirring the mixture after each 1 minute of cooking.

2 Stir the Muenster and Parmesan cheeses into the hot white sauce. When the cheeses are well mixed, gently toss the cooked pasta into the cheese sauce. Serve. (Or if you want to make it hard, sprinkle a bit more Parmesan on top and brown in a 350 F oven for 20 minutes. This isn't necessary to serve Mac and Muenster as a comfort food, but it works great for special occasions.) ❖

# EASY KIELBASA

MAKES 1¹/₄ POUNDS

## INGREDIENTS

1-2 feet hog casings

4 slices bacon, chopped

¹/₂ pound ground waterfowl

¹/₂ pound ground picnic roast

4 cloves garlic, minced

1 teaspoon salt

1 teaspoon pepper

¹/₄ cup cold water

1 teaspoon whole mustard seed

Real kielbasa is smoked a bit before it is cooked. For the harried cook, the bacon in this recipe will provide some of that smoked flavor. You can also intensify the smoked flavor by adding a handful of hickory chips to the charcoals before cooking.

### COOKING

1 Prepare the hog casings according to package directions. Grind the meats together through the coarse plate on the grinder. Then in a large bowl, add the garlic, salt, pepper, water, and mustard seed. Mix thoroughly by hand, and stuff into hog casings.

2 To cook, preheat the barbecue to medium heat, and just as you put the brats on add about ¹/₂ cup of hickory chips. Grill about 10 minutes a side, until all the pink is gone. ❖

---

### HOW SHALL I COOK THEE? LET ME COUNT THE WAYS

Once you case a sausage, you increase your choices of how to cook it. You can grill sausage, split and fry it in a pan, or slice it into chunks to add to soups, stews, spaghetti sauces, and chilies. Chorizo works great in chilies. Fennel and Parmesan Italian sausages are super in spaghetti sauces. And kielbasa, Polish, and bock sausage add spice to pea soups or stews. You can also put cased sausage in a skillet with water about halfway up the side of the casing, then simmer until all the water is gone, and brown gently to finish them off. This is my personal favorite.

You can also boil them. If you intend to boil the brats, dogs, or any other sausage, add 2 tablespoons of dry milk powder to each pound of sausage mix. This will give the cooked dog a smoother texture. And please notice that there are no chemicals in these mixes. Your finished dogs and brats will be the color of cooked meat: gray or brown, not red as with commercial dogs. If you can't live without the red, substitute Morton's Tender Quick for the salt in the recipe. About 1 teaspoon per pound of ground meats will provide the characteristic commercial color. ■

# POLISH SAUSAGE

MAKES 1 POUND

## INGREDIENTS

1-2 feet hog casings

$1/2$ pound ground waterfowl

$1/2$ pound ground picnic roast

2 teaspoons sweet paprika

1 teaspoon dried leaf marjoram

1 teaspoon dried leaf winter savory

$1/4$ teaspoon ground clove

1 teaspoon garlic powder

1 teaspoon salt

1 teaspoon black pepper

$1/4$ cup cold water

3 chunks hickory for smoking

You can cook this indoors in a large skillet with water, just as we did the Goose Bratwursts, but if you have the time, or it's just too hot to heat up the kitchen, water smoking will add a whole other dimension to the flavor.

### PREPARATION

1 Prepare hog casings according to package directions. Grind the meats together through the coarse plate of your grinder. In a large bowl, combine the meats with the paprika, marjoram, winter savory, clove, garlic powder, salt, pepper, and water. Mix thoroughly, then grind again.

2 Stuff the sausage into hog casings, twisting into 4-5 inch lengths.

### COOKING

1 Presoak the wood chunks about 30 minutes. Preheat water smoker, filling the reservoir with 3 quarts of water, then adding the hickory chunks to the coals.

2 When the smoker has reached 220-240 F, place the sausages on the cooking shelves, and cover the smoker. Smoke $2^1/2$-3 hours, or until all the pink is gone.

3 Serve with home-fried potatoes and good mustard. ❖

# BOCKWURST

MAKES 2 POUNDS

## INGREDIENTS

2-3 feet of hog casings
    (about 1¹/₂ inch diameter)
1 pound 10 ounces ground
    gadwall (or other dabbler)
6 ounces ground pork shoulder
¹/₄ cup minced onion
¹/₂ cup milk
1 egg, lightly beaten
¹/₂ teaspoon ground cloves
¹/₂ teaspoon ground sage
¹/₂ teaspoon ground mace
1¹/₂ teaspoons salt
1 teaspoon ground black pepper
2 tablespoons dried parsley
    flakes (or 2 teaspoons fresh)

If you like really luscious fatty sausages, you may want to alter this recipe and add the meats in equal portions. For the fat conscious, that's still about 30 percent fat. On the other hand, I like the occasional lean sausage. Just for a change. I think variety is what makes life more pleasurable.

### PREPARATION

1 Prepare hog casings according to package directions.

2 In a large bowl, combine the meats with gloved hands. Add the onion, milk, egg, cloves, sage, mace, salt, pepper, and parsley. Mix well with your hands. Refrigerate 1 hour and check flavor.

3 Stuff mixture into the casings, twisting into 3-4 inch lengths.

### COOKING

Drop into boiling water, lower the heat to simmer and continue cooking covered for 30 minutes. Or try one of my mother's favorite sausage dishes, which follows. ❖

# BOCKWURST AND FRIED POTATOES

**SERVES 4-6**

### INGREDIENTS

2 tablespoons oil

1 pound bockwurst,
  in $1/2$-inch slices

$1^{1}/_{2}$ pounds of potatoes,
  precooked and sliced

1 medium onion, sliced thick

1 green bell pepper, sliced

1 red bell pepper, sliced

1 cup beef bouillon

$1/2$ teaspoon red pepper flakes

1 teaspoon salt

$1/2$ teaspoon ground black pepper

There's nothing better than hot sausages on a cold night, except maybe for a one-dish dinner that's really easy to get on the road.

### COOKING

1 In a large skillet, heat the oil to medium-high heat and brown the bockwurst. Once browned, about 15 minutes, add the sliced potatoes, onion, and green and red peppers and stir, coating the vegetables well with the pan juices.

2 Add bouillon, pepper flakes, salt, and pepper to the pot, cover, and lower the heat to simmer. Cook about 15 minutes, until the green peppers soften. Serve immediately. ❖

**TIP** To pre-cook potatoes, arrange $1^{1}/_{2}$ pounds unpeeled potatoes in a circle in a microwave. Cook on high (700 watt)s for 12-15 minutes. Once cooked, cool to room temperature, then peel and slice.

# OVEN SALAMI

MAKES ONE 9-INCH-LONG, 2-INCH-DIAMETER SALAMI

## INGREDIENTS

10 ounces ground, skinless duck

6 ounces ground, skinless
   chicken

1 teaspoon Morton's
   Tender Quick

1/2 teaspoon salt

1 tablespoon brown sugar

2 tablespoons non-fat
   milk powder

2 tablespoons red wine

1 teaspoon whole black
   peppercorns

1/2 teaspoon whole
   coriander seed

1/4 teaspoon ground mace

1/5 teaspoon garlic powder

Make this easy lunchmeat from the legs and breasts of one average-sized mallard, or with a combination of diving duck breasts. It's a delicious way to stretch those birds further than you thought possible. If you have a problem finding mace or whole coriander, check your local health food store's spice selection or contact Penzey's Spices, Muskego, WI (414-679-7207).

### PREPARATION

1 The night before, combine the ground meats with the Tender Quick, salt, and brown sugar. Mix thoroughly by hand, cover, and refrigerate overnight.

2 At least 2 hours ahead, in a small bowl combine the milk powder and red wine. Stir until dissolved. Set aside. Crack the whole peppercorns and coriander seeds by placing in a plastic bag and rolling over them with a rolling pin (or wine bottle). Add them to the wine and powdered milk, along with the mace and garlic powder. Stir, then sprinkle this flavoring mixture over the meat and mix thoroughly by hand.

3 Shape into a roll, about 2-inches in diameter. Wrap in plastic wrap, seal, and place in the refrigerator to let the flavors mingle (2 hours to overnight).

### COOKING

1 Preheat oven to 200 F. Place the salami on a cookie sheet and set in the center of the oven. Bake about 5 hours, or until the center is no longer pink.

2 Cool on the counter, until the salami reaches room temperature, then store in the refrigerator up to 2 weeks. Slice thin to serve on sandwiches, or as a snack. ❖

# TRADITIONAL DRY-RUB JERKY
### 1 POUND FRESH MEAT MAKES ABOUT 3 OUNCES JERKY

**INGREDIENTS**

1 pound thinly sliced
   breast meat
1 teaspoon salt
$1/2$ teaspoon black pepper
$1/2$ teaspoon onion powder
$1/4$ teaspoon garlic powder
1 teaspoon brown sugar

Here's the best reason to own a meat slicer. If you make lots of jerky, and get frustrated at how long it takes to prepare, a meat slicer will improve your mood. It can slice thinner than most of us can, faster, and with less back-breaking labor. Then too, thinner slices cook faster. As usual for jerky, slice with the grain (for breast meat, that means slice long-ways).

**PREPARATION**

1 Spread out the sliced meat on a cutting board. In an empty salt shaker, combine the salt, pepper, onion powder, garlic powder, and brown sugar. Hold your hand firmly over the top and shake it up to mix the spices well.

2 Sprinkle about half the spice mixture over the meat slices, then press the mixture into the meat with the palms of your hands. Turn the meat over, and repeat with the rest of the spice mixture on the other side. With a meat mallet (or the side of a sturdy plate) pound the spice mixture into the meat, being careful not to tear the slices. Place in a resealable plastic bag overnight.

**COOKING**

1 The next day, preheat the oven to about 160 F. Remove the jerky slices from the bag and lay them across a metal grid in the oven. (I've used cake cooling trays or the metal grids from my smoker.) Prop the oven door slightly ajar to let the steam escape easily, and let cook about 3-5 hours, or until the pink is all gone and the meat is dry but not brittle.

2 Let the jerky cool to room temperature, then place in muslin bag and hang for 48 hours until all the moisture is gone. Store in glass jars, vacuum-sealed bags, or resealable plastic bags in the freezer or refrigerator. ❖

# MARINATED PEKING JERKY
## 1 POUND FRESH MEAT MAKES ABOUT 3 OUNCES JERKY

### INGREDIENTS

1/4 cup rice wine vinegar

1/3 cup soy sauce

1 teaspoon salt

1/2 teaspoon black pepper

2 tablespoons brown sugar

1/8 teaspoon anise seed powder

1 pound thinly sliced, skinless
   goose breast

For a little different jerky flavor, give this one a try. The vinegar and soy sauce will not only add flavor to the meat but will also tenderize it.

### PREPARATION

1 In a large, resealable plastic bag, combine the vinegar, soy sauce, salt, pepper, brown sugar, and anise seed powder. Seal, and shake to combine.

2 Dry the meat slices with paper towels, then add to the marinade in the bag. Shake the bag to thoroughly coat the meat, then reseal and refrigerate overnight.

### COOKING

1 Preheat the oven to 160 F. Remove the meat from the marinade without rinsing, and let it air-dry on a metal rack for 1 hour. (Use a cake cooling rack or clean racks from your smoker.)

2 Place the racks of meat in the oven and prop the door slightly ajar—a wooden spoon handle about 3/4 of the way up the door is about right. Cook 4-6 hours until the meat is no longer pink inside, and dry but not brittle.

3 Let the jerky cool to room temperature, then place in muslin bag and hang for 48 hours until all the moisture is gone. Store in glass jars, vacuum sealed bags, or in resealable plastic bags in the freezer or refrigerator. ❖

# WINGED PEPPERONI STICKS

MAKES 1 POUND OF MIX

### INGREDIENTS

**10 ounces ground, skinless waterfowl meat**

**6 ounces ground, skinless chicken meat**

**1½ teaspoons salt**

**½ teaspoon black pepper**

**½ teaspoon garlic powder**

**½ teaspoon onion powder**

**½ teaspoon crushed red pepper flakes**

**½ teaspoon dried leaf thyme**

**1 bay leaf, crushed**

There are two ways to get good-looking pepperoni sticks from ground meats. One is to freeze the pepperoni mixture on cookie sheets and cut them out. But the easier way is to shape them with a Jerky Master. It looks like a caulking gun but comes with two nozzles: one for making these pepperoni sticks, and one for ground jerky that looks like regular strip-type jerky but cooks much faster. And since there are no knives involved, maybe even the kids could make the jerky from now on. The Jerky Master (with metal cooking grid) is available for $29.99 from Hi Mountain Seasonings (800-829-2285).

PREPARATION

1 In a large bowl, combine the waterfowl and chicken meats. In a blender or small food processor, combine the salt, pepper, garlic powder, onion powder, red pepper flakes, thyme, and bay leaf. Process a few pulses until the bay leaf is in small pieces.

2 Preheat the oven to 160 F. Add the spices to the ground meat and mix thoroughly by hand. Refrigerate for 24 hours, to let the flavors develop.

3 To shape the sticks: Use a Jerky Master, or proceed as follows. Line a standard 10-15 inch cookie sheet with waxed paper. With your fingers, press the meat out on the cookie sheet, about ¼ inch thick. Place the cookie sheet in the freezer, level, with another sheet of waxed paper over the top, and let it sit about 90 minutes at 0 F. The meat should be solid but easy to cut.

COOKING

**1** Lift the partly frozen ground meat off the cookie sheet and transfer it to a cutting board. Remove the waxed paper. Now cut the meat into strips about $^1/_2$ inch wide and 6 inches long. Place the frozen strips on a metal grid and put it in the center of your oven. (I have used cake cooling racks for the metal grids, though an occasional weld comes loose. It doesn't effect the jerky.)

**2** Cook at 160 F about 5-6 hours, leaving the oven door slightly ajar to let steam escape easily, until all the pink is gone from the middle of the sticks. For the Jerky Master: Cook at 160 F about 2 hours, until the pink is gone from the middle of the sticks.

**3** For both methods: Remove the metal grids from the oven and let the sticks on them cool to room temperature. Then place in a muslin bag and hang for 48 hours until all the moisture is gone. Store in glass jars, vacuum-sealed bags, or resealable plastic bags in the freezer or refrigerator. ❖

# ERIC'S CAROLINA WATERFOWL JERKY

MAKES 2 QUARTS OF MARINADE

## INGREDIENTS

3 tablespoons ground coriander

1 cinnamon stick (about 6
   inches), chopped

1 star anise, cracked

1 whole clove, cracked

1 tablespoon garlic powder

2 teaspoons orange peel powder

1 tablespoon ground sage

2 fresh bay leaves, chopped
   (or 1 dry)

3 juniper berries, cracked

2 tablespoons chopped
   fresh ginger

1 pinch red pepper flakes

$1/2$ cup kosher salt

$1/2$ cup dark brown sugar

$1/2$ cup granulated sugar

2 tablespoons Tabasco

1 quart water

1 goose, or 2 ducks
   ($1^1/_2$-2 pounds boned meat)

I don't know too many graduates of the Culinary Institute of America who shoot their own birds and make jerky—among other things—out of them. But Eric Sharpe isn't the usual chef. If you like this, be sure to try his Cippolini Onion and Fresh Thyme Stuffed Duck Breast on page 68.

### COOKING

1 Combine all the ingredients, except the birds, in a large saucepan and bring to a boil. Turn the heat down to simmer, and simmer 5-10 minutes. Cool the mixture until cold, finishing the cooling in the refrigerator (so it reaches 45 F).

2 Slice the meat into strips $1/4$ inch thick and about 3-4 inches long. If the bird is tough, cut the meat across the grain. Remove excess moisture with paper towels, and place the strips in a large Crock-Pot, stainless steel container, or split between 2 resealable plastic bags (1-gallon-sized each).

3 Pour the spice mixture over the strips of meat. Mix thoroughly, making sure all the pieces are covered. Cover and refrigerate for 24 hours, turning occasionally.

4 Remove the strips from the marinade, and wipe any excess spice from the meat. Place in the oven on a steel drying grid, at the lowest possible setting (which usually is the low end of "warm," about 140 F).

5 Dry for 6-10 hours, checking every 30-60 minutes, so it does not become too dry. Jerky should be cooked (not pink inside) but not brittle. The rest is personal choice. Store in an airtight container up to 2 months. ❖

# MESQUITE-SMOKED JERKY
## 1 POUND FRESH MEAT EQUALS ABOUT 3 OUNCES JERKY

### INGREDIENTS

2 pounds duck or goose breast

$^1/_3$ cup sugar

2 tablespoons salt

1 cup red wine

1 medium onion, quartered

4 cloves garlic

1 whole canned jalapeño pepper

$^1/_4$ teaspoon dried leaf oregano

$^1/_8$ teaspoon ground cloves

$^1/_4$ cup sour cream

3 cups mesquite chips

### PREPARATION

1 Trim the breast meat. Slice thinly ($^1/_4$-$^1/_8$ inch thick) with the grain. For thinnest slicing, place the boned breasts on a waxpaper-lined cookie sheet, in the freezer for 1-2 hours, until the meat is firm but not frozen solid. Then slice.

2 In a blender or food processor, combine the sugar, salt, wine, onion, garlic, jalapeño pepper, oregano, cloves, and sour cream. Purée, and pour into a large non-corrosive bowl. Add the sliced meat and stir to coat the slices. Cover tightly and refrigerate overnight.

### SMOKING

1 Remove the meat from the marinade without rinsing and allow to air dry on paper towels for 1 hour. Meanwhile, put the mesquite wood chips in a bowl of water and let soak at least 15 minutes.

2 Place the meat on the smoker racks and turn the smoker on. Place 1 cup of mesquite chips in the wood pan at a time, until you've used all three cups within the first 2 hours of smoking. Then let the meat smoke another 8-9 hours. When done, the jerky will be dry to the touch but will bend without breaking.

3 Remove the jerky from the smoker and place in a jelly bag or small bag sewn from game bag fabric. Let it hang in a cool dry place, away from bugs, for another 48 hours, to finish off the drying. Store in the refrigerator or freezer in resealable plastic bags, vacuum-sealed bags, or in sealed glass jars. ❖

DUCK

&

GOOSE

# SMOKING

COOKERY

# OSAGE-SMOKED MALLARDS

MAKES ³/₄ POUND

---

### INGREDIENTS

3 chunks Osage orange wood

1-6 whole ducks, skin on
(whatever will fit easily in
your water smoker)

1 teaspoon bottled chutney
per duck

---

**TIP** Choose an apricot, peach, or pineapple chutney. Actually, any chutney that has an orange, yellow, or red color will do. Blue chutneys (blackberry or blueberry, for instance) make the finished ducks look odd and don't quite add the right flavor.

I don't know who invented the water smoker, but whoever it is, I'm grateful. Water smoking is the easiest way to smoke a pile of ducks, and you end up with moist, delicious birds that are a pleasure to share with your friends and family. And all you did was stick in the plug or light the propane—or if you were really energetic, fooled with a few briquettes. This most basic recipe is for dabbler ducks. For diving ducks, turn the page.

### PREPARATION

1 Two hours ahead, set the chunks of wood in a pail of water.

2 Thirty minutes ahead, set up the water smoker. Drain the wood chunks and nestle them into the fake coals. (If you are using charcoal briquettes to fire your smoker, heat the unit to 240 F before adding the chunks.) Fill the reservoir about ²/₃ full with water. Turn the unit on, place an oven thermometer inside, and heat to 220-240 F.

### SMOKING

1 Dry the ducks with paper towels, inside and out. In a small bowl, liquefy the chutney, in your microwave, about 10 seconds on high (700 watts).

2 Place the ducks breast up on the smoker racks, spoon the jelly across the breast and legs. Close the lid and cook for about 3-4 hours, checking the oven thermometer periodically to be sure you are maintaining 220-240 F.

3 At 3 hours, insert a meat thermometer into the thigh of the duck. It should register about 160-180 F when done. Remove from smoker and serve. I like these smoked ducks as an appetizer or snack, but if you prefer to make them a meal, serve with strong-flavored side dishes like red cabbage (see next recipe). ❖

# SAUTÉED RED CABBAGE

SERVES 6

### INGREDIENTS

1 slice bacon
1/2 cup red wine vinegar
2 tablespoons brown sugar
1 teaspoon salt
1 small head red cabbage,
cored and sliced thin

### COOKING

**1** In a large skillet, over medium heat, cook the bacon until done. Remove the strip of bacon and save. Combine the vinegar, sugar, and salt in a measuring cup.

**2** Stir the cabbage mixture into the drippings so it is well coated. Add the vinegar mixture and let the liquids come back to a boil. Crumble up the strip of bacon and sprinkle it over the cabbage. Reduce heat to simmer and cook about 15 minutes more. ❖

Shredded chips, small chips, and chunks are the most common forms smoking woods are prepared. The smaller the wood, the faster—and hotter—it burns. So for long smoking, like with water smokers, use the larger chunks; for a quick blast of smoke flavor during grilling, use a small amount of the larger chips. And for the first few minutes of dry smoking—so you get the smoke flavor in before the meat starts to cook—use the shredded chips.

# BEER-SMOKED SCAUP

SERVES 4

---

### INGREDIENTS

4 small diving ducks
24 ounces honey porter
2 cups water
2 teaspoons kosher salt
1 teaspoon pepper

---

It was the first year we hunted Druzilla, the retriever who wouldn't, and the first legal bird that crossed her path was destined to be shot. It was a lesser scaup. And she did not retrieve it. But smoked with beer, the scaup at least provided a tasty meal for the table. This is also a good way to fix any off-tasting birds.

PREPARATION

1 Leaving the skin on, bone the breast meat from the carcass. Each bird should supply about 4 ounces of meat, from both sides of the breast. Dry the meat with paper towels.

2 Pour the porter into a deep bowl or resealable plastic bag, then add the breasts. Marinate overnight in the refrigerator.

SMOKING

1 Remove the breasts from the marinade, and pour the marinade into the aluminum-foil-lined reservoir of your water smoker, along with an additional 2 cups of water. Start the water smoker and preheat to about 220-240 F.

2 Pat the duck breasts dry with paper towels. Carefully roll them up, overlapping the skin by an inch, and fasten with a wooden skewer. (Try to roll the skin so it covers all the breast meat, stretching it if necessary.)

3 Season with the salt and pepper, and place the rolled breasts over the water reservoir. Then close the lid. Cook 1-1$^1$/$_2$ hours, or until the reservoir is about dry. Serve as an appetizer or as a main course with corn on the cob and chilled watermelon slices. ❖

# HICKORY-SMOKED WHOLE GOOSE WITH ORANGE CURRANT MARMALADE

SERVES 4-6

## INGREDIENTS

3 cups hickory chips
$\frac{1}{2}$ cup orange marmalade
$\frac{1}{2}$ cup red currant jelly
1 5-pound goose

This recipe was specially designed for use with a Little Chief–type dry smoker. I recommend the smaller model smoker (for making 25 pounds or less), which provides a constant low temperature for this particular recipe. Then, once you've infused all the smoke into the bird, tightly wrap it up in foil and transfer it to the oven to finish the cooking. That will keep the meat moister than if you finished it in the smoker.

### SMOKING

1 Thirty minutes ahead: Cover the hickory chips with water and allow to soak 30 minutes. Then place the marmalade and the red currant jelly in a microwaveable bowl. Microwave on high until the jellies liquefy, about 1 minute. Stir well to combine, and chill.

2 In a Little Chief–type dry smoker, place the goose in the center of the smoker and smoke for 3 hours, using the moist hickory chips 1 cup at a time.

3 Remove the goose from the smoker and wrap in aluminum foil. Place it in a preheated oven at 350 F, and cook another 40 minutes until the meat thermometer inserted in the inside of the thigh (careful not to touch bone) registers 140-145 F for medium-rare, or 150-155 F for medium. Serve either hot, or chilled overnight, with the orange currant marmalade. ❖

# WATER-SMOKED GOOSE

INGREDIENTS

3-5 chunks hickory wood
1 tablespoon red currant jelly
    per goose
1-4 geese

You'll need a whole goose, with the skin on, for the best results when water smoking. Since I'm basically a lazy person, I prefer electric or gas to operate the smoker. But charcoal smokers work just as well. Keep the temperature about 240 F, the water reservoir full, and the smoker will do the rest. As for the jelly glaze, it's not crucial. But it adds a little flavor and makes the skin crisp nicely, for a beautiful and tasty treat. I chose red currant here, but you can use orange marmalade, jalapeño, or homemade chokecherry and prickly pear cactus jelly. Relatively tart jellies, in other words—not the sweet ones.

PREPARATION

1 Two hours ahead, set the hickory chunks in a pail of water to soak.

2 About 40 minutes ahead, set up and preheat the water smoker. Drain the wood chunks and place them over the hot coals. Add about 3 quarts of water in the reservoir (at 240 F you will have 3 hours of water), and place the reservoir over the coals. Set the cooking grates over the water.

COOKING

1 In a small bowl, liquefy the jelly, 10 seconds in a microwave at 700 watts. Set aside.

2 Rinse each goose with cold water inside and out and dry with paper towels. Brush the jelly glaze all over the birds.

3 When the smoker is at 240 F, place the bird(s) in the smoker. (You can use both cooking grates, just leave space between the birds for the smoke to circulate.) Cover the smoker and cook $2^1/_2$ hours.

Reglaze with the liquefied jelly and cook another 30 minutes.

 **4** To serve, let cool about 10 minutes, then carve like a Christmas goose. Or bone the breast off the carcass, and run through a meat slicer. Then you can make sandwiches with piles of thinly sliced, delicately smoked goose meat, ripe tomatoes, salt, and pepper. Then spread a mixture of half mayonnaise and half horseradish (2 tablespoons each should be enough for 4 sandwiches) on the bread for the perfect finish. ❖

# SUCCULENT SMOKED DUCK

FOR 3 DUCKS

## INGREDIENTS

3 ducks

### FOR THE BRINE
$1/4$ cup non-iodized salt
$1/4$ cup brown sugar
1 teaspoon whole peppercorns
1 teaspoon onion powder
$1/2$ teaspoon garlic powder
$1/2$ teaspoon ground mace
$1/4$ teaspoon ground coriander
1 cup apple cider
$1/2$ cup Madeira
$1^1/2$ cups water

2 cups apple wood chips

The Succulent Smoked Duck stays that succulent partly because of the marinade. But the other factor is letting the bird finish cooking in the oven—wrapped in foil to protect all those delicious juices. Those inexpensive dry smokers are great, but I prefer how moist my birds are with this two-step process.

### TO BRINE
1 Trim the fat and all rough edges off the duck. Dry with paper towels.

2 In a large resealable bag, combine the salt, sugar, peppercorns, onion powder, garlic powder, mace, coriander, apple cider, Madeira, and water. Shake to mix. Add the ducks and brine overnight in the refrigerator.

### TO SMOKE
1 Preheat a dry Little Chief–type smoker (140-160 F). Put one cup of the apple wood chips in the chip pan, place the ducks in the smoker, and close the door. After 45 minutes, pour another cup of chips in the pan and continue smoking for a total of $2^1/2$-3 hours.

2 To finish off the duck: Place in a 300 F oven for 40-50 minutes, or until inside temperature is 170 F (by a meat thermometer). ❖

# TWICE-COOKED DUCKS

**FOR 3 DUCKS**

### INGREDIENTS

3 cups maple chips
3 whole dabbling ducks

### MARINADE

1 cup red wine
1/3 cup sugar
1 teaspoon dried onion flakes
1 teaspoon dried oregano leaves
1/2 teaspoon ground cumin

This recipe may seem totally backward—smoking a duck *before* the marinade. But it's a delicious way to ensure a rich infusion of smoke into the meat, while still crisping the skin and preserving all the delicious juices.

### SMOKING

1 Trim birds, then rinse and dry with paper towels. Smoke in a Little Chief–type smoker (140-160 F) for 2 hours with 3 cups maple chips, smoked one at a time. Remove.

2 In a resealable plastic bag, combine the wine, sugar, onion, oregano, and cumin. Shake to mix. Add the cooled duck and shake the marinade all around it. Place in the refrigerator and marinate overnight. ❖

### GRILLING

1 Start the barbecue on one side of the grill. Heat to medium-high (about 550-600 F).

2 Place the duck on the un-fired side of the grill and put the lid on. Grill until internal temperature is about 170 F (by a meat thermometer), about 40-45 minutes. ❖

# SMOKED MEATLOAF

SERVES 6-8

---

### INGREDIENTS

3 chunks hickory

1 medium onion, chopped

$^1/_2$ green pepper, chopped

4 cloves garlic, diced

$^1/_2$ teaspoon salt

$^1/_2$ teaspoon ground black pepper

2 tablespoons sour cream

1 egg

1$^1/_2$ cups Italian flavored
 bread crumbs

1 teaspoon chicken bouillon

$^1/_2$ cup hot water

$^3/_4$ pound ground duck or
 goose meat

6 ounces ground chicken

---

Smoked Meatloaf may take a bit longer to cook than the more traditional layered meatloaf you cook in your oven, but once you try this moist, delicately smoked variation, it will become a regular part of your too-hot-to-cook-in-the-kitchen repertoire.

AHEAD
Two or more hours before you want to start cooking, place the hickory chunks in water.

PREPARATION
In a large bowl, combine the onion, green pepper, garlic, salt, black pepper, sour cream, egg, and bread crumbs. Combine the bouillon granules and hot water, and when dissolved add that to the mixture. Mix well. Add the ground meats and mix thoroughly with your hands. Transfer the mixture into a barbecue-proof loaf pan.

COOKING
1 In an electric or propane water smoker: Drain the wood chips and set them on the coals, then fill the reservoir with water. Place the meatloaf, uncovered, in the center of the lower rack. Cover the smoker. Start the smoker. For propane, set on medium heat. (If you are using a charcoal water smoker, start 30-35 briquettes in a chimney, then when they are ash-covered, place in cooker at same time as the meatloaf. You'll need to add approximately $^1/_3$ more unstarted coals every 45 minutes.) For all three you need to maintain a temperature of 220-240 F for a total of 2 hours.

**2** Cook for 60 minutes, until the meatloaf has shrunk away from the sides of the loaf pan. Cover the top of the meatloaf pan with a length of foil, and gently turn the meatloaf over into your palm (with a hot mitt, for protection). Set the loaf pan aside, and tip the meatloaf back onto the cooking grate, with the same end up. It will hold together well, with a little care. If you are nervous, just set the meatloaf down on the foil. Cover the cooker and continue cooking the meatloaf another 60 minutes.

**3** Remove the meatloaf carefully from the smoker. Let sit 10 minutes, then slice thick to serve hot, or chill for a cool summer dinner. Hot, I like to serve it with garlic bread and mashed potatoes (made with half white or russet, and half sweet potatoes); cold, it makes a great sandwich, with a little mustard. ❖

# FIVE-BY-FIVE SMOKED DUCKS WITH HORSERADISH SAUCE

MAKES 2 MALLARDS

## INGREDIENTS

1/2 cup Morton's Tender Quick

1/4 cup brown sugar

1 teaspoon whole black peppercorns

1 bay leaf

1 teaspoon whole cloves

1/2 teaspoon whole allspice

1/2 teaspoon whole coriander

1 quart hot water

2 mallards

2-3 quarts cold water

Here's a smoking recipe for those of you who own those heavily insulated, Fort Knox–type smokers (nothing goes in, nothing goes out). This smoker costs more than the Little Chief–type smokers, but it allows you to smoke the bird completely without having to finish it off in your kitchen oven, and it keeps the meat very moist without extraneous work on your part. You can also smoke in cooler weather (though at 0 F you need to add about 20 percent more smoking time), thus extending your smoking season. In Montana, and other states that tend to have more than their fair share of winter months, that's a very good thing. And waterfowlers, it also means you can smoke fresh birds in December, for Christmas presents—not 4-month-frozen birds in May.

### TO BRINE

1 Combine the Tender Quick, brown sugar, peppercorns, bay leaf, cloves, allspice, and coriander in a quart jar of hot water. Cover the jar tightly. Keep it on the counter, shaking every 5-10 minutes until the salt and brown sugar have dissolved. Pour the brine into a 5-quart Crock-Pot. (Or other non-corrosive container: Glass will also work. No aluminum or plastic.)

2 Check out the ducks. Pluck any errant feathers, trim rough edges, and check once more for any organs left in the body cavity. Rinse with cold water inside and out, and place in the Crock. Add enough cold water to cover the birds, then stir them around gently to mix the brine. Submerge the birds below the brine with a small plate, then lay a piece of plastic wrap on the brine's surface. Place the Crock on the bottom shelf of the refrigerator.

**3** Brine in the refrigerator (at 38 F) for 5 days, rotating the ducks about every 12 hours to keep the brine well mixed. On the fifth day, take the ducks from the brine, rinse in cold water, and set them on a rack (over a drip pan) to air dry, one to two hours. They're done when the skin feels slightly sticky.

### TO SMOKE

**1** Prepare the smoker according to manufacturer's directions. My Cookshack smoker recommends lining the bottom with foil (leaving the drain hole open) and setting a small (2 ounce) chunk of dried wood in the wood box, but it does not require preheating. Check your own insulated smoker for details.

**2** Set the birds in the smoker, either hanging by a hook and string, or just sitting on a shelf mid-oven. Close the smoker. (Because a small amount of smoking residue and moisture from the meat will drip from the bottom of the smoker, place a drip pan under the smoker with a small rock to weigh it down on windy days, or place the smoker on a non-flamable surface that can be easily cleaned.

**3** Smoke at about 225 F for 5 hours. The internal temperature of the ducks will be about 150 F (tested with a meat thermometer), and will rise another couple of degrees before it cools. This is cooked enough. The red color you notice when you slice into the meat is from the brining mixture.

**4** To serve, mix 1 tablespoon of cream-style horseradish with 3 tablespoons of lingonberry preserves (or any other tart preserve, like whole cranberry sauce or elderberry or chokecherry jams) for each duck served. Slice the duck thin or thick, and dip into the sauce. ❖

# PLUCKING BIRDS

There are only two good times to pluck birds. The best time is right after shooting them. As long as you can still feel some body warmth through the skin, the feathers will pluck as easily as they ever will. But almost as good is after they've been properly aged. Anywhere in between is more like pulling teeth than feathers.

You can start plucking on the third day the bird has aged on the bottom shelf of the refrigerator. Better yet is to wait 5-6 days, when aging is about optimum. Test the bird's feathers by gently pulling at some of the shorter feathers along the spine, or down on the lower belly below the vent. If they don't pull easily, put the bird back in the refrigerator and test it again in 24 hours. But don't wait more than 7 days at 33-38 degrees. And don't test the bird's breast feathers. In fact, don't start plucking the first bird of the day right in the middle of the breast. Start somewhere where the yips and jerks of forgotten technique and rusty or arthritic fingers won't be noticed when the bird is presented at the table. And don't pluck a bird when it's in rigor mortis. Depending on temperature, this is anywhere from 12-48 hours after the shot. To check for rigor, just bend a leg at the knee. If rigor is not present, the joint will bend easily. If it is, the joint won't give at all, nor will the feathers.

Let me add, right here, that there's nothing wrong with skinning a bird rather than plucking it. A lot of recipes in this book—and in fact, many of the most popular recipes among waterfowlers—don't require a plucked skin to make the dish work. On the other hand, for some dishes it is not only traditional to use a whole plucked bird, but actually much better. Barbecuing, roasting, and smoking whole birds, for instance, are best done with the skin on, whether that bird is a teal, mallard, or goose. And many people wouldn't cook a breast without the skin on. The skin keeps the meat moister in all methods of dry cooking, and if the bird is fresh (i.e., not a year or two in the freezer) the skin will be delicious.

## PLUCKING VS. SKINNING

Here's the reality of plucking: In some states, at any given time, your local game department may issue an advisory regarding the safety of eating wild birds. I have seen recommendations, in various places and times, to eat no more than one dabbler per week or one diver per month. Some research suggests that removing the skin and innards eliminates the contaminants, making your birds safer to eat. There are a lot of factors involved, state to state, so check with your local game department before your season starts. ■

# BREASTING AND PLUCKING IN THE FIELD

Any bird will pluck easily right after the kill, while the body is quite warm. And with birds for which you only need retain the breast, it is a simple, quick, and expedient method to care for the birds.

This is the method my friend Judy Cornell likes to use for teal, and she is very quick at it. (See complete photo sequence on pages 138-139.) As soon as the bird hits the ground, Judy lays it breast-up, feet toward her, on a piece of dry land. Starting at the center of the breast, she takes small bunches of feathers between her thumb and index finger and pulls firmly upward. Once she has a clear spot, she takes the feathers as close to the skin as possible, using her other hand to steady the skin and keep it taught as she plucks. Then when she has the entire breast plucked, she uses her poultry shears to separate the entire breast, meat, rib cage, and sternum (breastbone) in one piece, from the rest of the carcass—except to leave one feathered wing for ID naturally attached until she gets it home. This method avoids having to draw the bird, and lightens the load not only in the field but on the way home. By lifting the breast off the carcass, she has also eliminated any chance that the internal organs might taint the meat. And she is so quick at it she doesn't lose but 3 minutes a bird from her hunting time.

After freeing it from the carcass, Judy pops the breast into a resealable bag, which she slides into her game vest. Then, when we are back at the vehicle, she puts it on ice. She will then age it in her refrigerator when she gets home, in the resealable bag, before eating it. (See pages 5-6.)

If you need to retain the legs (as with mallards and larger birds), or legs and wings (as with geese), I've always found it easier to just half-draw the bird, then take everything home and care for it there. That's just one of the reasons I've grown so attached to the water bath method of plucking birds. Because usually, by the time you get the birds home they're cold, and while dry plucking aged birds is pretty fast, it's nowhere near as easy as the water bath method.

# PLUCKING BIRDS IN A WATER BATH

Aside from liking to age my birds in-feather, and liking the convenience of a sink and a little rock-and-roll while I'm cleaning birds, there's another reason my methods are so different from Judy's. It's simply inherent in where we like to hunt.

Judy enjoys walking the prairie from pothole to pothole jumping ducks. One duck, one pothole at a time. I live near a big waterfowl nesting area and a large reservoir on the Upper Missouri River. I love to sit quietly in a blind, waiting for the birds to come to me. Our resident population of wildfowl is very well educated as to where we hunters might be sitting. So the greater part of

my harvest shows up at the kitchen sink in a bunch, when the northern birds—who haven't had time to figure out where every local nimrod in every local puddle likes to hang out—start migrating through. It's feast or famine.

If I manage to get one or two of the resident birds, I'll hand pluck them, then age the

No matter how you choose to pluck the birds, the result is about the same. From left to right: A mallard plucked immediately after the kill; a mallard dry plucked after aging 6 days; a mallard plucked with a Duck Naked machine after aging 6 days (the shine came from my impatience and getting it a bit too close to the fingers); and last, a mallard plucked by water bath method after aging 6 days.

plucked bird in a sealed plastic bag. But I've found that when I have a bunch of birds to pluck, aging first, followed by the water bath, makes the job much quicker. When the birds are flying, it's better to have a shotgun in hand than a poultry shear.

For ducks and small geese, half-fill a large soup or canning pot with water and start it over high heat. If you have a 50,000 BTU Camp Chef stove and a nice day, do it outdoors. Otherwise, start the pot on the kitchen stove. When it gets to the point where it looks like the water is about to boil—you'll see small bubbles start to form on the bottom of the pot (or check with a candy thermometer: it should be about 212 F)—turn the water down to simmer and stir in 1 teaspoon of liquid dish washing detergent. Cover the counter next to the pot with several layers of newspaper.

Now, holding them by the neck, two at a time, gently lower the birds into the water and stir around for 12-15 seconds. Raise the birds and check to see if the lower belly feathers pull easily. Shake as much water off as you can, then lay each bird on the newspaper and let it cool just enough to handle. The feathers should almost roll off the skin.

Water bath plucking is a method I learned from Norm Strung, and over the years I have found that it works better for ducks than for geese. The larger goose needs a larger dipping pot to allow them to float as freely in the solution as the ducks do. I've tried turkey frying pots and canning pots, but find that while some areas of a goose will pluck more easily dipped, some areas don't get as much effect. The system is ideal for all ducks, however.

Why does it work? The detergent neutralizes the oil on the feathers, allowing the hot water to penetrate to the feather butts and loosen them from the hide. The trick is to not apply the heat too long or let the bird cool off completely before plucking it. The first time you try this method, dip one bird for 10 seconds at 212 F, then take it out and see if the breast feathers pull easily. If not, add 3-5 seconds to the dip. But don't go much over that: too much heat will only set those feather butts as if in concrete.

## WHICH BIRDS SHOULD YOU PLUCK?

Over the years, I've discovered that most hunters don't pluck all their waterfowl, nor do they leave them whole. No big surprise here. Plucking a whole bird takes time—especially if you want it to look right. Skinning and breasting a bird is fast, easy, and takes up a lot less freezer space. But at least once in a while you need to pluck a whole bird. How else will you get to serve that great 7-course roast Christmas goose dinner?

What we do at our house is pick a handful of the least damaged birds for plucking whole. That ends up being a couple of Canada geese and a handful of mallards and teal. These are also the best birds—in our region—for dry roasting, smoking, and barbecuing. If I had a brant handy, I'd leave that whole, too.

The problem is you can't always tell from the outside. Check for blood on the feathers, then bend the legs at the knees and hips, and the wing at the shoulder. (Check your regulations: At this time, according to Montana state game regulations, I need to keep the wing on any bird as large or larger than a goose. Recommendations are offered by the feds, but individual states fine-tune them, and a recent call to my game warden pointed out that by "wing" most—but perhaps not all—states mean the first bone of the wing. That's the humerus: the bone that goes from shoulder to elbow.)

If everything's okay at the joints, and there's no blood on the breast feathers, I'll start plucking the breast. If the skin is intact there, that bird gets the royal treatment. Any bad joints, or more than one or two pieces of shot in the breast, and I'll just part it out.

The thing is, if the bird is fairly shot up, it not only doesn't look good whole on the table, but it may not age well. In that case, it's best to breast the bird out and use Arnie's brine bath method to treat bloodshot meat. Skip the aging process. Nine times out of ten, you'll end up chunking or slicing the meat for a long, slow moist cooking method anyway, so you'll have a chance to remove bone fragments, imbedded feathers, and shot pellets while you're preparing the meat for the pot. Soup and chilies are perfect dishes to tenderize un-aged birds.

## MODERN TECHNOLOGY

The other easy method for plucking birds is an automated plucker. The initial investment is higher ($200 and up), but unlike the waterbath method, all the mess is kept outdoors. (You'd be amazed how far feathers can travel—and how long after the season is over they show up again.) And for those of us who are getting a little arthritis in our hands, electric plucking machines are a real advantage. Hand plucking two geese in one day, wet or dry, leaves my hands more than a little sore the next day.

Powered pluckers are available with vacuum attachments, or with an air-draft system that deposits feathers into a bin. But don't kid yourself: No matter how you pull feathers out of that bird, wet or dry, they will be everywhere. If you don't live in a house where everyone participates in the hunt, it's best to take the plucking outdoors.

Which is the best system? It depends on you. My friend Tim used to have an automated plucker. It became so popular with his friends that he had to charge fifty cents a bird just to keep up with the replacement "fingers." He just bought a new vacuum-equipped plucker, and I asked him how he liked it. His response was that the water method was just as fast, and just as "clean"—for both the duck and the area around the duck cleaning. It was just his own preference to keep the whole mess out-of-doors. I just got a Duck Naked plucker, and I agree. It's a joy to use most days of the season— less wear and tear on my hands, and a lot less mess—but on those late-season northern-tier, finger-freezing days I still prefer the warm kitchen.

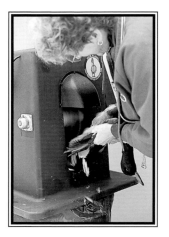

The author making fast work of a mallard. When you use this powerful tool, follow safety instructions, and don't leave apron strings loose.

Keith, our 13-year-old chocolate Lab, may be retired but he still likes to help out.

# STEP 1
## PLUCKING THE BREAST

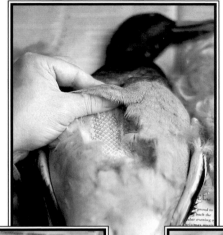

1 Starting at the breast, with the duck's feet firmly held in your off hand, pinch a few feathers between your thumb and index finger and roll or pull them gently but firmly. If they pull hard, reduce the number of feathers taken in each pull.

2 Pluck up to the neck feathers, then across the breast, wing to wing.

3 Pull the feathers with thicker veins one at a time to prevent tearing the skin.

4 When you have the breast rough-plucked, move down to the legs.

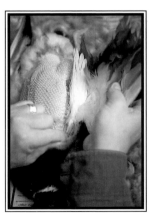

5 Lift the wings and pull them out to the side. Pluck the larger feathers here, up to the shoulder joint.

# STEP II
## PLUCKING THE BACK

1 Turn the bird on its breast, and holding the feet in your off hand, pluck the back.

2 Pluck the back from the tail to the neck feathers.

# STEP III
## PLUCKING AND TRIMMING THE LEGS

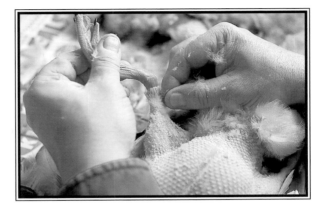

1 With the bird on its back again, pluck the legs.

2 The feathers on the lower leg are quite short. Do your best here. When you're done, you can sear the leftovers with a candle or butane kitchen torch.

3 Take the bird's leg in one hand, and bend the knee joint back hard enough that the bones just break through the skin.

4 With a knife or poultry shear set between the upper and lower leg bones, clip through the ligaments.

5 Clipping between the lower and upper leg bones keeps the bird's leg bone—and your dinner—free of bone chips.

# STEP IV
# TO REMOVE THE SHOULDER JOINT: DUCKS

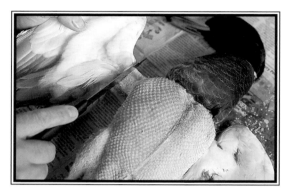

1 Pluck the feathers of the wing, about 1-2 inches from the shoulder joint. This will leave a nice flap of skin for a more attractive table. Cut through the skin and muscle around the upper arm bone at this point.

2 Slide the knife into the shoulder joint, freeing the upper arm bone from the muscle.

3 The humerus or upper arm bone meets both the clavicle, or wish bone (in the front of the bird), and the scapula or shoulder blade (in the back). Twist the humerus a half turn, and slice through the muscle.

4 Slide the shears into the joint, between the humerus and the clavicle and scapula. Clip the ligaments that hold the shoulder together.

5 Remove the wing and cover the opening with the flap of skin.

# GOOSE WINGS
## A VARIATION ON STEP IV

1 Pluck the goose wing down to the elbow. Feel for the joint between the upper wing (humerus) and the lower wing bones (radius and ulna). Place a chef's knife or meat cleaver into this elbow joint.

2 Cut through the skin and ligaments attaching the humerus to the radius and ulna.

3 A clean cut with a chef's knife or meat cleaver is the quickest way to deal with wings.

# STEP V
## REMOVING THE HEAD AND TAIL

1 Pluck the neck feathers out about 3 inches from the base of the neck. With a chef's knife, cleaver, or poultry shears, cut the neck 3 inches from the base. If you like, gently press the loose neck skin down and clip further down on the spine. Keeping that extra neck skin makes the duck or goose look nicer at the table.

2 Press your fingers down into the arch of the pelvic bones to make them stand up clearly.

3 Cut the tail off about $1/2$ - $3/4$ inch beyond the pelvic arch.

4 Note that placing the cut here assures that you will avoid perforating the lower digestive tract and tainting the meat.

# STEP VI
# DRAWING, RINSING, AND THE FINAL TOUCHES

1 Make a slit in the lower belly skin to allow complete drawing of the bird. Be as conservative as you can, but allow room for your fingers to do the job thoroughly.

2 Gently grab the end of the intestines and draw the digestive tract out. Then feel inside for liver, heart, lungs, etc. Remove the esophagus and crop from the neck end.

3 Rinse the bird until the water comes clear. Drawn completely, the water will flow unimpeded.

4 With a butane kitchen torch or candle, sear the down and wisps of feathers you couldn't get before.

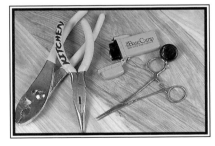

5 A pair of regular or needle-nose pliers or the hemostat from your fly-fishing vest make handy tools for pulling recalcitrant pin feathers. A lighter can be used to sear down remnants, too.

# JUDY'S METHOD
# BREASTING TEAL

What makes my friend Judy's method so fast and easy is everything you don't have to do—like plucking the whole bird, drawing the whole bird, and splitting and splicing joints. You name it, she's probably eliminated it. That's why it's such a fast and easy method to handle those birds for which you only need save the breast. Like teal. (Check your local regulations.)

As you prepare to remove the sternum, keep in mind that the sternum of a duck is shaped more squarely than that of a domestic chicken. It's also more bony than cartilaginous. This is probably why ducks fly better, and avoid the frying pan much more successfully.

**1** Pluck the top of the breast. (This can be done when the bird hits the ground, or after aging 3-5 days.)

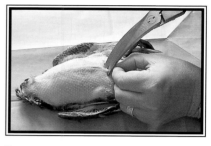

**2** With your fingers, feel for the bottom edge of the sternum. Make a small slit just through the skin and stomach here. (You'll be able to see the vitals, but take care not to puncture the intestinal tract.)

**3** Insert the tip of the shear into the slit. Starting at the middle of the lower end of the sternum, cut through the skin and membrane, freeing the breast meat and sternum. Turn the corner of the sternum, and cut between the ribs and sternum where it is only cartilage joining them together.

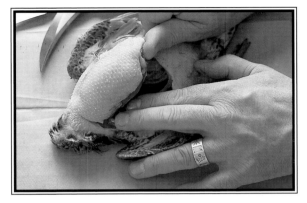

4 Here, one side of the breast has been freed from the carcass.

5 Return to the bottom of the sternum, and cut up the other side in the same way.

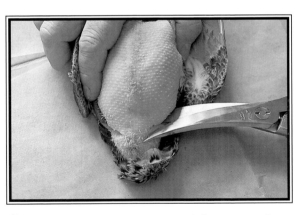

6 Clip through the cartilage and skin across the top of the sternum. Rinse and dry the back side of the sternum. (Most of the time, the heart stays attached. You'll need to pluck it from the sternum before rinsing.)

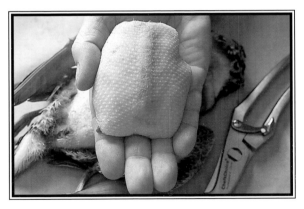

7 Once done, the entire breast comes free, making a delicious cut of meat to roast, broil, or grill.

# QUICK & DIRTY:
## BONING-OUT SKINNED BIRDS

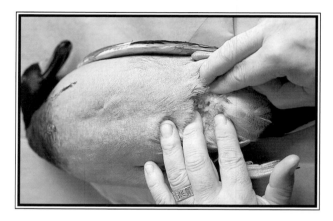

1 Lay the bird on a clean surface, with the feet toward you, and find the vent.

2 Keeping your knife forward of the vent (because you're not going to draw this bird, there's no point opening the cavity), pinch some skin up and make a small slice across the skin.

3 Slide your knife point into the cut and, with the blade pointed upward, open the skin at the top of the breast.

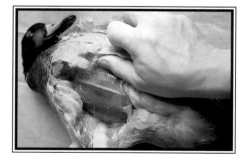

4 With your thumbs under the skin, press the skin away from the breast on both sides of the bird.

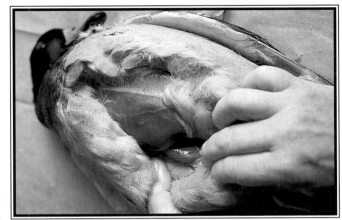

5 Press your thumbs down inside the skin, down toward the leg. Expose the leg.

6 Pull the skin off the thigh and drumstick, exposing the leg all the way to the hip.

7 Holding the carcass firmly, grasp the leg at the knee, and press the top of the leg bone (the femur) out of the hip socket. You'll see a ball on the end of the femur when it pops out of the socket.

8 Separate the thigh and drumstick from the carcass by slicing parallel to the body, across the thigh meat.

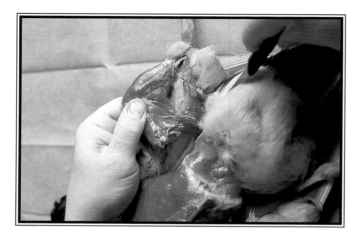

9 As you cut, keep your knife between the carcass and the ball at the top of the femur. Repeat with the other leg, and set both legs aside.

10 Starting at the center of the sternum, cut the breast from the carcass.

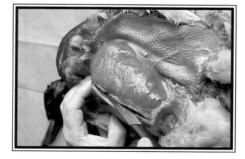

11 Slide the knife down against one side of the breast, keeping the knife tightly against the breast bone (sternum) so as not to waste any meat.

12 Scrape the breast meat from the side of the breast bone (sternum).

**TIP** In these pages, whenever the list of ingredients includes a breast (singular) of duck or goose, it is the whole chest area of one bird. Where breast is plural (breasts) it refers to plural birds as well. I know; it looks weird: You bone a breast and you have two very distinct pieces. But technically, biologically, it is still just one breast.

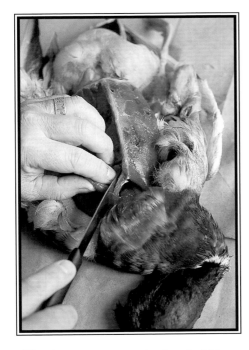

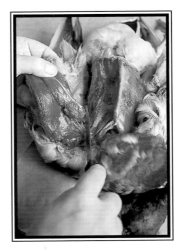

**13** When you get to the front of the breast, the wishbone (clavicle) will be in your way. The wishbone lies arched at the top of the breast.

**14** Slice down the inside and outside of the wishbone to free the breast meat.

**15** Once free of the wish bone, slice the breast meat free of the carcass at the shoulder.

**16** A typical young mallard (about 2¹/₂-3 pounds) will provide about 8 ounces of breast meat when breasted in this way.

# WRAPPING & FREEZING

The trouble—and pleasure—with the wild ducks and geese we bring home from the blind is that they are fat. Not as fat, certainly, as the commercially raised variants of our wild birds, but they're fat enough to cause problems. Any fat in the freezer, be it pork, beef, venison, or goose, spoils faster than lean meat. At first, say after 3-4 months, it may just seem that the ducks you are cooking now aren't as good as the ducks you cooked a month ago—and they were all from the same flock. But don't start avoiding them: The longer they sit in the freezer, the worse it's going to get.

The good news is that there are ways to slow down this process of deterioration. Whatever wrapping method you use, there are several easy steps to good game storage.

Get out all the air you can when you wrap it, and keep out all the air you can in storage. Wrap tight, wrap double, and eyeball the condition of your wrap jobs when you retrieve other meat from the freezer. Arrange your birds in chronological order—oldest stuff in front (or on top), newest stuff buried (cook the oldest stuff first), so that you don't handle the packages a lot during storage. The less handling, the less chance of tearing or rubbing. And if a package does start to show wear, cook that bird next.

Let's get started. There are lots of choices you need to make to ensure that your ducks and geese bring you as much pleasure at the table as they did the day you carried them home from the blind.

## WHAT'S THE BEST WAY TO FREEZE BIRDS? WHOLE OR IN PARTS?

Whole birds are particularly prone to holes developing in the packaging over the course of freezer storage, simply because they have wings and legs. A package of elk steak, double wrapped, has no projections. Whole birds do. Every time the package rocks and rolls in the freezer, every time you dig through the bird section looking for a package of green-winged teal breasts, those sharp elbows and knees rub against the paper and eventually poke a hole through the envelope, letting in air. And then of course, since these are wild birds taken by shotgun, there are sometimes rough edges.

Parted-out birds are by definition smaller pieces of meat with a greater exposed outside surface area than protected inside layer. To put it another way, there is more skin surface (even if you've taken the skin off) than thickness to the meat in parted-out birds. Thus skin is in contact with the air. And skin, whether it is the skin itself or the outer layer of the meat masquerading as skin, is the first thing that gets freezer burned.

On small birds like teal, if the entire outside of the bird gets freezer burned you've lost a very large percentage of meat. A goose breast would lose a smaller percentage of meat. But the point is to wrap so you don't lose any meat. Air may be the single most necessary element for life, but the frigid, dry air of your freezer wreaks havoc on stored birds.

Are you ready? You've plucked, skinned, parted, and rinsed, now take a moment and choose your method: paper, plastic-with-foil, or vacuum seal.

Here I am at my optimistic best, starting a teal bag with only one teal breast. Wrapping each breast in it's own separate plastic wrap packet is a great way to keep the cook's options open. You can take out half, or a third, or just one bird breast out of the bag at any time, without having to semi-thaw and pry apart individual servings, which often tears delicate meat.

## WRAPPING WITH FREEZER PAPER

Freezer paper is great stuff. But it lacks flexibility. That doesn't mean you have to forsake that most inexpensive of wraps. You just need to wrap in two steps.

**FOR PARTED BIRDS:** When packing up skinned breasts, tightly wrap together in clingy plastic wrap as many as your family will eat in one meal, creating as uniform, dense, and thick a package (either square or rectangular) as possible. Then wrap again in freezer paper. Cut a long enough piece of plastic wrap that you can wrap the breasts snug. Then with both palms at the same time, press the air out to the sides, and fold the ends over the middle. Cut enough plastic wrap so that it is long enough to make one or two wraps, giving you 2-3 layers of protection on every surface of the meat.

Follow the same routine with legs, whether skinned or not. Place as many as your family will eat in one tight pile. Then wrap tightly in plastic, pressing out the air, before flapping the ends over. The clingier the plastic wrap the better it is for the meat—though the harder for the wrapper. The goal with breasts or legs is to make the package as compact as possible, which also helps create a shape that will stack efficiently. Stacking individual packages snugly provides one more barrier against air...and makes it possible to store more meat in less space.

Now take the plastic-wrapped package of breasts or legs and place it on one end of a length of freezer paper, long enough to make $2^{1}/_{2}$ turns around the meat. Pull the near end of paper over the meat, tuck the end under the package snugly, and roll the whole package once completely. Press the air out of each side of the package, fold the ends envelope-style across the package, and roll one more time. Fold the end flap into a triangle—like the flap on an envelope—and tape it shut.

**FOR WHOLE BIRDS:** In parted birds the plastic wrap seals the air out very effectively. Whole birds are another story. The plastic wrap still forms a sleek protective layer on the outside surface of the skin—or, if skinned, on the meat itself—and serves to tuck in sharp elbows and knees to make a more compact package. Yet there's that pocket of air in the body cavity the plastic wrap can't touch. If the rib cage is intact—no broken ribs, no torn cartilage—then the bones, cartilage, and connective tissue that make up the rib cage will protect the breast meat from freezer burn. A shot-up rib cage, however, will expose the meat, and unless eaten within 2-3 months, these birds are probably best parted out.

To wrap whole birds, lay the plastic wrap on the counter and lay the bird lengthwise on it. With one hand, tuck the legs as close into the body cavity opening as possible and wrap the bottom half of the bird snugly. If the bird is large enough to

Whether you need to freeze the moisture for vacuum packing, or just want to keep your breasts and legs from freezing into a solid mass, place the parts on a cookie sheet, and place in the freezer for 2-3 hours.

save the wings, press them tightly against the breast. Snug them down with the wrap. Once these limbs are secure, make a tight wrap around the bird, pressing the edges of the plastic wrap down to make a good seal.

For the outer layer, cut a length of freezer paper about three times the length and width of the bird. Center the bird on one end of the paper, crossways. Wrap the near end of the paper tightly once around the bird, pulling the package toward you as you work. Now wrap it around the bird again. With the palm of your hands, press as much air as possible out through the sides. Then fold the sides of the paper tightly against the carcass. Roll one more time. Then fold the end of the freezer paper like an envelope flap and tape it down securely to the package.

Now, no matter how hard you tried, paper will not totally conform to the irregular shape of whole birds, so it is important to take some time to tape-tighten any loose pockets. When you are done, the package should be an obvious bird shape. Squeeze it all over. If you feel give (air pockets), press the paper down against the body and tape it more securely. If there are large pockets, you'd best start over.

# PLASTIC ON PLASTIC:
## USING RESEALABLE FREEZER BAGS

Anyone who knows me or my cookbooks knows that I also do a variation on the plastic wrap theme for legs. Admit it: Legs aren't like breasts. You can take two mallard breasts out of the freezer, marinate them half an hour, and throw them on the grill for a delicious dinner. But breasts and legs—while probably created equal—don't end up equal. Legs are tough. Usually, very tough. And a problem for the cook.

What happens at our house is that I'll collect legs all season, all types, all sizes—from Canada geese to rooster pheasants—and store them in batches large enough to make a Crock-Pot-full all at once. And I start early. As soon as the first bird falls, I pull out a gallon-sized heavy-duty, resealable plastic freezer bag, and label it Legs or Betty Grable Bag. Something obvious. Then each time we clean our birds, I wrap each pair of legs in clingy plastic wrap and drop it into the bag. The individual wrap keeps the legs easy to separate, so they'll be easier to thaw. It also protects the early birds from freezer burn until I've got enough legs to cook. Then a Crock-Pot full of Let Them Eat Legs or Tender Mole Legs is a painless way to tenderize that most troublesome—and neglected—of bird parts.

This is a also a great way to store bird parts that are going to be used within one to three months. If you need to store your birds longer, use one of these other methods to protect the birds from the freezer.

## WRAPPING WITH FOIL

My friend Jim Gelhaus prefers to make his second layer aluminum foil. And having dined on at least one two-year (in the freezer) bird, I can tell you it is quite effective at keeping air out.

Jim starts by wrapping carefully with plastic wrap as above, but then adds a double-long length of heavyweight foil. He first wraps the foil loosely around the bird twice to be sure he has a good double-layer on every surface. Then he presses the foil against the carcass so it conforms perfectly to the bird. This is a much tighter outer package than paper can achieve, but you need to be more careful of foil in the freezer. It will tear more easily than paper. Placing foil-wrapped birds in a paper grocery sack provides a little insurance.

# VACUUM SEALING

This is my favorite method of packing birds for the freezer. Right now I've got mallard breasts and whole mallards in my freezer that have been there 3 years—vacuum sealed—and they look, and taste, as fresh as the day I packaged them. But you need a high-quality sealer with heavy bags that will stand up to the rubbing that the projections on whole birds will inflict on them, as well as provide good protection from the cold dry air of your freezer. I've tried a couple of vacuum sealers. The Food Saver runs $150-$300, depending on the model, but is the best I've used.

The only trick to vacuum sealers is that you need to contain the liquid during sealing—either wrapping the whole or parted-out birds first in plastic wrap, or semi-freezing the birds or parts before sealing. The package simply won't seal if liquid is working its way out of the bag during processing.

To plastic wrap first, just follow the previous instructions for whole and parted birds, but use a single layer of wrap. You don't need the extra layer for freezer life. The Food Saver bags will provide that. You just need to trap the moisture. Or, if you have a little more time and a bit of freezer space, you can also semi-freeze the birds in your freezer and avoid the plastic wrap step.

For keeping birds in the freezer a long time, without losing quality, a good vacuum sealer is unbeatable. It's also faster than any other method I've used.

I prefer to semi-freeze the birds. That breaks the job into two steps, about 2 hours apart, a break long enough to make dinner and put your feet up for a while. And it takes less time overall, which is always a good thing.

First, dry the whole birds or parted-out legs and breasts with paper towels, just enough to keep the excess moisture from running on the cookie sheets, and place the meat on a waxed paper–lined cookie sheet or any metal pan. Metal conducts cold best, freezes the birds more quickly. (Be sure to wipe the inside of whole birds with paper towels, too, so there's not a puddle of water frozen inside the bird for the next year.) Cover the whole or parted-out bird loosely with another piece of waxed paper, and set the sheets in the freezer, 2-3 hours at 0 F. This will allow any lingering water or blood to solidify. Be sure to prop the cookie sheet up level and leave a little space between the birds and/or bird parts so they'll get good air circulation. If you are freezing a lot of birds at one time, you can layer your cookie sheets, just separate each layer by propping ice-cube trays, a previously frozen package of meat, or some lightweight object at each corner. (A lakeside lodge I stayed at used cork floats to separate their freezing trays very effectively.) Pre-freezing parts before packaging is also a help to the cook: The parts will separate quite easily when thawing for dinner.

The birds are ready to pack when you can pick them up from the cookie sheets and, like a piece of sturdy cardboard, they don't flop over.

# DROPPING IT IN THE FREEZER

Whichever method you use to wrap your waterfowl, use a permanent marker to write down the type of bird, date taken, and what parts are to be found in the package in large, easy-to-read letters. If your final layer was aluminum foil, mark the information on a piece of masking tape and wrap it securely around the package.

Because I often cook breasts and legs separately, I prefer to sort my parted bird packages into breast packages and leg bags. The leg bag is often large, with a variety of species in it, because I cook legs a Crock-Pot-full at a time, foraging on them over a long weekend. Breasts are wrapped in 8-ounce packages, or at least as close to that as I can get. We are a family of two, so 8 ounces is one meal. If you have a larger family, wrap so that you have a minimum of 4-6 ounces of meat per person per meal. As you sort and wrap, keep in mind that larger packages are more freezer efficient, because there is less outer surface to get freezer burned.

Then arrange the meat in the freezer by species or cut, so that it can be found easily. At our house, we make a habit of creating compartments in our chest freezers. They're not fancy. In fact, mostly we use 12- to 18-inch-square cardboard boxes

## DULL DUCK KNIVES

There's nothing that slows down bird care like a dull knife, and with waterfowl it seems that your knife gets dull as soon as you use it. It isn't just your imagination. Waterfowl have tougher skin and more fat than any other bird we hunt. That combination just dulls knives. The only trick I know to combat this is to keep the sharpening tools handy. Every few strokes on the bird, tune up the blade with a ceramic or steel rod. When that's not enough, I turn to the sharpening stones.

The other thing that works for me, if I am parting out a bird completely, is to always start out with a minimum of one very sharp boning knife, one semi-sharp skinning knife, and a pair of sharp poultry shears. The skinning knife kept half-sharp is handy for cutting through the membrane between skin and muscle, without accidentally slicing up the meat. It's the same principle as with skinning deer. Saving the actual slicing of meat and cutting through ligaments for the very sharp boning knife will extend the life of the edge; and the shears separate joints, cut through rib attachments, and trim rough edges with less wear and tear on my hands than a knife. ■

that are tall enough to reach the rim of the freezer. Each box is a category: usually either the species or the cut of meat.

We divide the bird section into upland and waterfowl; waterfowl into whole or parted. And place whole birds in paper shopping bags, 2-3 to a bag. Layer upon layer upon layer of protection, all geared to handle, turn, drop, shuffle, or shift these precious packages as little as possible—and keep their envelope sealed.

Then once a year, usually at the end of summer, we defrost the freezers and re-order the packages chronologically: oldest packages on top, newest on bottom. We have two freezers, so when we defrost them in August we consolidate all the meat from hunting seasons past into the freezer upstairs, off the kitchen, and arranged it so the newest stuff is on the bottom of each compartment, the oldest on top. Then, any new animals we are lucky enough to bring home that hunting season get put in the sparkling clean—and empty—downstairs freezer. This usually keeps us honest. But the year we put a buffalo in the downstairs freezer, we ended up getting a lot of aerobic exercise. Stairmasters, we called ourselves.

The aim is always to keep the meat tasting fresh and sweet. Freezers should be kept at 0 to -5 F; opening kept at a minimum. Chest freezers are better than uprights. Old meat should be eaten before new. And Mother's Day is just one of many great occasions to enjoy a roast goose.

# THE FREEZER

For years I took it as a matter of faith that chest freezers were better than uprights. Part of the reason was that my husband said they were. And I believed him because his theory seemed to be absolutely logical. If cold air falls and hot air rises, then it stands to reason that every time I opened the freezer compartment on top of the refrigerator—an upright refrigerator—the cold air would fall (out into the room) and be replaced by room air, 70 degrees and warmer.

We own two chest freezers, plus a refrigerator-freezer, and depend on game meat stored in those appliances for 356$\frac{1}{2}$ days a year. So a couple of years ago, I decided to see just how accurate my husband's logic was and put his cold-loss theory to the test.

In preparation, I placed a refrigerator/freezer thermometer deep inside each freezer for half an hour with the door closed. This allowed the thermometer plenty of time to get an accurate reading of optimal closed-door temperature. Then, with a stop watch in hand, I opened each freezer one at a time and marked how long it took for the temperature gauge to start rising. The freezer over my refrigerator was a snap: it took exactly 15 seconds for the temperature to start sprinting upward, and very quickly looked more like Marion Jones than a cubic appliance. My two other freezers, both chest-type units, were absolutely earth bound—and boring. Truth is, I quit timing them after 4 minutes with no change on the thermometer.

What this means for you as a hunter is that when your chest freezer keeps your precious game meat at a constant -5 to 0 F, that game tastes fresher and lasts longer than the game meat your hunting partner stores in an upright whose temperature pops up and down like a plastic bobber every time he opens the door. Plus, the harder your freezer works to achieve and hold 0 F, the higher your power bills. And money given to Montana Power, PG&E, and Con Ed is less money in our pockets for bismuth, tungsten, and steel.

Carrying this out to its logical conclusion, the best system for storing meat is to have at least one chest freezer that is rarely opened, with a second, more accessible freezer where you can transfer and keep meat for 2-3 weeks at a time. As I've mentioned before, we have taken this to an extreme, with two chest freezers. The one in the basement is emptied in late summer and all old meat moved upstairs. All new meat goes downstairs, and once we are done hunting we simply don't open the downstairs freezer except when we run out of steaks or roasts upstairs. Then we open it once to grab a sack-full of meat at a time. And since the downstairs freezer is also sorted and categorized, it's easy to get in and out of in 4 minutes or less.

Chest freezers rule! And since waterfowl have more fat than almost any other wild game animal, chest freezers rule big time for waterfowl hunters.

## FREEZE TIME

The other measure of success in freezing ducks and geese for the table is freezing them quickly. This keeps the texture of the meat as prime as possible. If you bring home 1-2 birds a trip, no problem. But if you are subject to the wings and arrows of outrageous migration, you need to keep track of how long it takes to freeze the birds. If you get really lucky, having more than one freezer is an advantage.

According to freezer guidelines, at -5 to 0 F, which is the recommended temperature for storing any meat for extended periods, you should only try to freeze $1\frac{1}{2}$ pounds of meat for each square foot of freezer space at one time.

In a fifteen-cubic-foot freezer, for instance, you can freeze 22 pounds of meat at one time. Boned out, a mallard breast weighs about 8 ounces; a whole freezer-ready lesser Canada or snow goose weighs about 2-6 pounds. Make an estimate of your total freezable meat, wrapped up and freezer-ready, and if you're close to $1\frac{1}{2}$ pounds per square foot, double-check it on the bathroom scale.

To speed freezing, use the hanging baskets that come with most freezers. They allow the best air circulation and will hold 2-3 whole geese, with space between for good air circulation. Second best is metal trays and cookie sheets. Metal freezes instantly, thus multiplying the freezing action. You can also spread the fresh-wrapped meat out across the top of what's already frozen, leaving at least one inch of space between the new, unfrozen packages so nothing but cold touches the new meat. If you have time, you may also want to rotate the packages every 6 hours so they'll freeze more evenly and quickly.

# CLARKE'S LAW: IF IT CAN GO WRONG, IT WILL GO WRONG AT MY HOUSE

Every now and then I make a big mistake. The last one was last spring when I decided that I didn't have time to pluck the snow geese we'd brought home from South Dakota. I went downstairs to the basement freezer and found I had enough room to just drop the birds in whole, so I did. Big, big mistake. And the only thing I can say in my defense was that it sounded like a good idea at the time.

Six months later, I was cleaning out the freezers for the new season, and there were seven whole snow geese staring me in the face.

I'll tell you right off: The mistake wasn't that the meat suffered. Those feathers were as good at insulating the meat from freezer burn as they had been at keeping the snows warm while cruising at 25,000 feet above our decoys. The problem was that I had planned to pluck them—which was why I'd left them whole in the first place—but, after several months in the freezer, they wouldn't pluck. My old-reliable water bath was a bust. The skin tore like wet paper at the slightest touch of the electric duck plucker. And dry plucking was like pulling teeth.

Something had happened to change the relationship of those snows' feathers to their skin. I struggled through hand plucking the first four. Then, with hands and back aching, I was forced to skin and bone out the last three. I could have done that last March. Given the suspicious nature of those snows and the long periods between in-range shots, I had lots of free time in the blind to pluck birds...and save myself a lot of trouble.

So I learned a lesson, and pass it on. If you plan to pluck, don't freeze them first as I did, expecting to do them later, one at a time, at your leisure. And if you plan to bone, just do it.

## THAWING

There was a second problem dealing with the Magnificent Seven Snows: Frozen inside a winter's worth of feather, they took forever to thaw. Well, seven days, and that included leaving them out on the counter for the first 8 hours to give them a head start. That's at least twice as long as it takes a naked bird to thaw. And a quantum leap over what the "experts" say is normal.

The standard rule in mainstream cookbooks is to allow 2 hours per pound (for birds under 5 pounds) to thaw birds in the bottom of the refrigerator. But I've never found that to work. Most Canada geese we take in Montana are lesser Canadas that weigh about 2 pounds, oven-ready. In 4 hours they are still frozen, even if I allow them to sit on the counter at room temperature—which would be a no-no anyway if the bird could actually thaw completely in that little amount of time.

I suspect wild meat is denser than commercial meat, since the birds are also older. I also suspect that when this timetable was developed, refrigerators were not so cool, nor freezers so absolutely cold. I'm not sure. It could also just be a typo that has lived forever. What I do know is that it takes 48 hours (and sometimes a little more) to thaw a 2-pound Canada in the bottom of the refrigerator. (That's 24 hours per pound, at about 38 F.)

Don't have 48 hours? Well, there are some safe, and not-so-safe ways to speed up the process. Let's start with the not-so-safe ways, and why it is best to do at least the final thawing in the refrigerator.

Whether you are talking wild or commercially raised birds, they all have bacteria in their systems, and all bacteria are inert when frozen. If you allow a thawed bird to sit at room temperature for 30 minutes, these bugs wake up. To protect both the flavor of the bird and the health of your family, it is best to thaw all birds, slowly, in the refrigerator.

Take a thermometer and check the bottom shelf of your fridge. It should read about 38-40 F. At that temperature, you can safely thaw your goose or duck, whole or in parts, until it is ready to cook.

Having said that, I'll admit that over the years I've used at least three shortcuts. Carefully. Those three are the microwave, the kitchen counter, and a large pot of cold water. I will use the microwave, once in a while, for complete thawing, but the counter and pot are simply a head start at the beginning of the process. Let's start with the last two.

To speed up the thawing process, place the bird in a plastic bag, then in a large high-sided pan, while still wrapped from the freezer. Allow it to sit at room temperature until the skin starts to thaw. You should be able to press your thumb into the breast and feel almost no give. At 70 F, this takes about 6 to 8 hours. As soon as you feel the slightest bit of give, transfer the goose (in a drip pan) to the bottom shelf of the refrigerator.

For vacuum and plastic sealed birds: Leave the bird sealed in the bag, and submerge it in a deep pot half-filled with cold water, about 2 hours. Again, when the flesh can be indented with little pressure, transfer to the refrigerator to complete the process.

## THAWING IN THE MICROWAVE

When you live in a house with two freezers full of game meat, you learn the advantages and disadvantages pretty quickly. The disadvantage is that everything you cook has to be thawed first, hopefully in a safe manner, every day, 365 days a year. Lose your patience with thawing in the bottom of the refrigerator, and it can end up just full of the seeds of food poisoning.

The advantage is you have a freezer (or two) full of meat. And a microwave oven. With care, thawing occurs so quickly in the microwave that germs don't have enough time to develop. But the microwave can also cook your dinner, before you're ready to cook it. To prevent this, make a habit of thawing only at reduced speed (about 245 watts, or the defrost setting) 2-3 minutes at a time for whole geese, 1-2 minutes at a time for smaller birds. After each 1- to 2-minute thawing cycle, place your hand on the meat, checking the extremities first. If you feel warmth anywhere, stop and let the meat cool again. And if there is any sign of cooking, stop immediately. Any sign of paler or opaque flesh or skin means you need to slow down. Done carefully, that should not happen.

Maximum time you can allow for this process? Thirty minutes of thawing and resting (both count on the timer). If it hasn't thawed in 30 minutes, place the bird back in the refrigerator and let it finish thawing there. For moderate-sized packages of boned meat, this is plenty of time to go from rock solid to completely pliable, with no health risk to you. And done slowly and cautiously, as directed, there is no risk to the bird taste and texture, either.

A 2½-pound mallard, ready for the oven, will thaw with 10 minutes of defrost wattage, using this off-and-on-again method. Allowing for resting time between each 2 minutes of defrost wattage processing, you're still well within the 30 minutes total.

The next question is how thawed does it need to be? For most cooking, a whole bird does not have to be absolutely thawed. The more thawed it is, however, the more evenly it cooks, the more moist it remains, and the less time it takes. But in a Crock-Pot, for instance, or in a pot of soup, if the bird parts are 80 to 90 percent thawed, that's enough. And if a whole bird is thawed enough that you can remove the final bits of innards, that is enough for most cooking methods.

Frying, however, demands absolutely thawed meat. It's a safety issue. If the bird hits the hot oil, either whole or parted out, when those last little drips of blood and water thaw instantly, and suddenly, directly into that hot oil it can spatter and burn you badly. This would be true of any meat: furred, finned, or feathered, commercial or wild. If you are going to fry it, make sure the meat is totally thawed. And, once thawed, if you can't dry the surface of the meat completely with paper towels, a light dusting of flour or cornstarch will protect you from spattering. This is a traditional way to not only dry meat for frying, but to add a thickener to the sauce.

As cooks of wild game we are always going to be more challenged in the kitchen than people who cook only commercially raised meats. But for me that's one of the joys of cooking game. From the moment that bird fell out of the sky, its taste and quality have been in my hands. With careful field care and good freezing and thawing technique, that bird is still as good as it was. Hopefully, better. Now it's up to the hunters to put on their aprons and choose the recipes that fit their lives and their tastes. A quick Wednesday night dinner for two, appetizers for New Year's Eve, or a very traditional stuffed holiday goose for family gatherings, it's time to put the shotgun down and get cooking.